Winning the Addiction Battle

God's Plan for Getting Your Life Back

Jim Watson

It is easy to go down into Hell; night and day, the gates of dark Death stand wide; but to climb back again, to retrace one's steps to the upper air - there's the rub, the task.
Virgil
http://www.brainyquote.com/quotes/quotes/v/virgil392882.html

Unless otherwise indicated, all Scripture quotations are from The Holy Bible, English Standard Version® (ESV®), copyright © 2001 by Crossway, a publishing ministry of Good News Publishers. Used by permission. All rights reserved.

THE HOLY BIBLE, NEW INTERNATIONAL VERSION®, NIV® Copyright © 1973, 1978, 1984, 2011 by Biblica, Inc.™ Used by permission. All rights reserved worldwide.

"Scripture taken from *The Message*. Copyright © 1993, 1994, 1995, 1996, 2000, 2001, 2002. Used by permission of NavPress Publishing Group."

COVER PHOTOS: "Images Used Under License from Shutterstock.com"

COVER DESIGN: Chris Scardina-OpenSkyDesign.net

Jim Watson Missions
P.O. Box 10281
Knoxville, TN 37939

www.jimwatsonmisssions.com
http://winningtheaddictionbattle.com

Copyright © 2016 Jim Watson
All rights reserved.

Title ID: 6069855
ISBN-13: 978-1530036295

I dedicate this book to my wife. Tammy has been my companion and friend since 1988. She is the love of my life. Because of her faithfulness to God and to me, she has experienced an extremely difficult and sometimes dangerous life. She is the real champion in all my stories.

This book is not intended to be a substitute for the medical advice of a licensed physician. The reader should consult with their doctor in any matters relating to his/her health.

This book is designed to provide information and motivation to our readers. It is sold with the understanding that the publisher is not engaged to render any type of psychological, legal, or any other kind of professional advice. The author shall not be liable for any physical, psychological, emotional, financial, or commercial damages, including, but not limited to, special, incidental, consequential or other damages. Our views and rights are the same: You are responsible for your own choices, actions, and results.

ACKNOWLEDGMENTS

I wish to thank Voyle Glover for encouraging me to write this book after hearing me preach a sermon on the topic.

A special thanks to Dave Goff, a friend since 1977, for proofreading this manuscript. Thank you for your suggestions and corrections. Thank you also for being my Barnabas. You were there for me at some of my most difficult moments. You helped others believe in me even when I could not believe in myself.

Thank you Kimberly Marsack for proofing this manuscript and for your many valuable suggestions.

Thank you Tammy Watson for encouraging me to finish this book and for reading this manuscript at least five times. I could not have done it without you.

Table of Contents

Dear Reader 1
Why Read this Book 3
My Journey of Helping People Change 7
Recovery: Just Don't Do it for Yourself 11
Part One: The Road to Recovery................................. 18
    Four Ways Your Addiction Can Ruin Your Life 21
    Mindsets that Cause You to Relapse 27
    How Relapse and Failure Can Help You 34
Part Two: The God Connection 46
    It All Begins With Christ 47
    God's Purpose for Your Life 55
    Part Three: The Image of Christ 59
    Quit Drinking the Poison of Unforgiveness 60
    Changed by Your Service to Others 64
    Humility and Recovery 71
Part Four: Surrender and Change 83
    Worship and Surrender... 84
    More Thoughts on Surrender 90
Part Five: Change University 98
    Your Thinking Needs to Change 103
    Developing a Vision for Change 112
    Relationships Can Help You Change 120
    Time is on Your Side 126
    Train yourself to be Godly 132
Part Six: Action Steps for Beating Addiction 143
    Action Step One: Connect With God 145

Action Step Two: Take Responsibility for Your Life 149

Action Step Three: Find a Church 152

Action Step Four: Develop a Daily Devotional Plan 155

Action Step Five: Start a Mastermind Group 165

A Call to Action 168

Suggested Books 170

    Devotional 170

    Success 171

About Jim Watson 172

Dear Reader

If you are reading this book, my heart goes out to you. Addiction to alcohol or drugs may have a stranglehold on your life. More than likely, you are afraid. If you are not scared, you should be. If your addiction has not already ruined your life, it eventually will.

However, I want to begin this book by giving you hope. The addiction that has gripped your life is not impossible to beat. You are not a hopeless case. You can defeat your habit and chase it from your life. Not only that, you can recover the life your addiction stole from you. You can still have a life again.

I know this from personal experience. It is not some theory I learned in school. I discovered it the hard way. Alcohol nearly destroyed my life. Most of my friends wrote me off as a hopeless case. However, when I gave my life to God, he gave me a new life, a life beyond anything I ever dreamed of attaining.

What God did for me was not an isolated case. My experience was not unique. Over the past twenty-seven years, through the Christian ministries founded and managed by me, I have seen God make some incredible changes in the lives of hundreds of men and women who ruined their lives because of addiction. With his help, they broke the chains of substance abuse and got their lives back. He can do the same for you.

Please do not be afraid of all my talk about God. I tried to do it without God. The results were always the same—failure.

Centuries ago, a man named Augustine wrote down these words:

"You have made us for yourself, O Lord, and our hearts are restless until they find their rest in you."

Inside of you and me is an emptiness that nothing but God can fill. You have tried to fill it—drugs, sex, relationships. For the most part, they left you empty and unhappy. They were unable to provide lasting satisfaction for the deep longing in your heart for something meaningful and durable. Some things can bring you temporary happiness, but in the end, they all come up short. Does that sound like addiction to you? You can never get enough. You always need more.

- Since all your efforts to eradicate your addiction from your life has thus far proved fruitless, please keep an open mind about God. He may be your only chance.
- If you are already a Christian, I will show you how to reconnect with God and get your relationship with him back on track.

I have written this book to share with you a proven method for helping you change your life. If you fully put into action everything I tell you, you will get your life back. If you do not, you give me no choice but to cancel my guarantee. You cannot just go partway and expect a complete result. In the addiction world, almost means relapse, pain, and self-destruction.

God has a bigger plan for you than the life of an addict. Perhaps you are ready for that new life. Experience has taught you that you cannot live this insanity any longer. You want to wake up from your nightmare. You want to regain your self-respect.

Today is your day. It is about to happen. Can you taste your new life? Can you picture what it can look like without addiction? Are you ready to begin? Today could be the first day of a brand-new life for you.

Why Read this Book

If your addiction to alcohol or drugs has not wrecked your life yet, it will. It will destroy your relationships, reduce you to poverty, introduce you to the criminal justice system, rob you of your self-respect, and, for some of you, put you in an early grave.

In your fight to regain your life, stalemates are rare. In this war, there is only one victor—you or addiction. You are not engaged in a play battle. It is a life-and-death struggle. You must win this war. If you are defeated, it will be the end of you—your dreams, hopes, and plans.

If you are tired of seeing your life wrecked by alcohol or drug addiction, this book can have a dramatic impact on your future. Be honest. Do you have a strong desire to change and be set free from the curse of addiction? In moments of sincere soul-searching, are you able to see clearly how your present lifestyle has frustrated your attempts to live a significant life? Have your problems and failures worn you down? Have you learned to settle for a life of limitations, lies, and manipulation?

It does not have to be that way. God has a bigger plan for you than addiction. In Jeremiah 29:11 (ESV), the Bible says,

> *"For I know the plans I have for you, declares the LORD, plans for welfare and not for evil, to give you a future and a hope."*

His plan for you and me is that we become like his Son Jesus.

> *"Now the Lord is the Spirit, and where the Spirit of the Lord is, there is freedom. And we all, who with unveiled faces contemplate the Lord's glory, are being transformed into his image with ever-increasing glory, which comes from the Lord, who is the Spirit."*
>
> II Corinthians 3:17-18 (NIV)

The battle plan for freedom from addiction is rooted in personal change brought about by your relationship with God. Only the power of God can permanently eliminate addiction from your life. Without the help of God, you will have no choice but to fight this battle using your strength and willpower.

You cannot win your battle with addiction using your strength.

Willpower, gritty determination, or effort will not change you. Only the actions of God in your life can produce lasting change. In this book, you will learn:

- How addiction ruins your life
- How personal habits, attitudes, and behaviors can prevent recovery
- A step-by-step plan to beat addiction
- A plan to help you get your life back

If you are content with your progress in life, then perhaps you are not ready for this book. This book is only for men and women who want a revolution in their life. A normal life for you is not the goal of this book. I want to show you how to live an extraordinary life, a life of impact, filled with meaning and purpose. If you do not want to change and defeat your addiction, put the book down. Please do not waste your time.

If you are still reading, that means that you have decided to defy the odds and do battle with the curse that has brought nothing but pain and suffering to your life. Deep down, despite all your relapses and setbacks, you must still believe you have a future.

Remember this: When you find yourself surrounded by hopelessness, discouraged by your circumstances, and skeptical about ever getting your life back, you should not be afraid. Help is on the way. God knows you better than you know yourself. He sees your trouble, feels your heartache, and hears your cries for help. Do not give up on your life. God has not given up on you.

"And call for help when you're in trouble - I'll help you, and you'll honor me."
Psalm 50:15 (The Message Bible)

Over the years, I have met many men and women who have surrendered their lives to failure and pessimism. Because of the disheartening condition of their lives, they believed they could never escape the prison they had built for themselves. They felt lost and powerless, condemned to a life of unhappiness and regret.

In addition to their personal sense of failure, feelings of rejection and haunting suspicions that God had deserted them tormented their thoughts and emotions. "God no longer cares about me," they cried. "If he did, why is this happening to me?" All their attempts to think positive thoughts and remove themselves from their predicament ended in frustration.

Perhaps you understand their feelings and disappointment. You are now going through something from which you cannot escape. Maybe, because of your addiction, your business is failing, and you are powerless to stop it. Perhaps your marriage is over, flushed down the toilet, without any hope of reconciliation. Whatever your personal tragedy may be, you feel stuck, like in quicksand. If help does not come soon, your life is over. You have run out of options.

Addiction is the Father of Personal Disaster.

Fortunately, God is not afraid when He sees you face down, struggling to breathe with dirt in your mouth. Your condition does not frighten Him. Whatever life throws at you, one thing you can know for sure: God is stronger than your circumstances, addiction, and weakness. Nothing has happened in your life beyond the power of God to repair. In the midst of all your mess, he still has a plan for you.

Since God has not given up on you, why should you throw your life into the abyss? After all, he specializes in using men and women, who have failed, lost their way, wrecked their lives, and trapped themselves in inescapable dead ends. His plan for you is bigger than your failure. Do not lose hope. Help is on the way.

I encourage you to read each page of this book prayerfully. Do not skim or skip.

My Journey of Helping People Change

If you are like most of us, you have found that real, lasting change is almost impossible. Change is often like a New Year's resolution—it rarely lasts. In my life, I have experienced a great deal of personal dissatisfaction with myself. I was not a bad person, well, maybe not entirely good either. I just found it impossible to live a life consistent with my expectations. Even worse, I was such a failure as a Christian. The standards outlined in the Bible were mostly beyond my reach.

I had two choices. I could just give up and accept myself as I am. Most people take that route. Accepting yourself as you are is one of the prevailing views of our culture. "Embrace who you are!" is the battle cry for most of us. Of course, that means we have to accept the consequences of being ourselves. For me, the potential results from making that decision were too awful for me to embrace with any seriousness. I decided to take a different path and figure out what I needed to do to make changes in my life.

Eventually, my journey led me to a life-ministry of helping men and women who had wrecked their lives because of their addiction to drugs and alcohol. I have been on that path for the last twenty-seven years.

At the beginning of my journey, a man who had spent twenty-five years of his life working with addicts approached me with some advice. I know he meant to be helpful; perhaps he wanted to fortify me for the impossible battle I was about to face. He said, "Don't expect much in the way of results from those people. Most of them will never get well."

His advice was not helpful. It discouraged me beyond measure. Here I was, at the beginning of a great adventure; I was about to begin a new ministry that I hoped would have a significant impact on men and women who had lost their way. Instead of providing encouragement or sharing tips that would help me succeed in my new journey, the best advice he could or me give me was, "Don't be discouraged by your lack of results." If he was right, that meant I would end up wasting my life working with people who were beyond help.

My first thoughts were, "How can this be? What does that say about God? Was he trying to tell me that God's strength was not powerful enough for the needs of most addicts?" After much prayer and thought, I concluded that either the Gospel message we proclaim was false, or our application of it was defective. Since I knew that the problem could not be God, I figured it had to be our methods, our understanding of how people change and become the men and women God always intended them to be.

His advice also did not correlate with my experiences. At a younger age, my addiction to alcohol had completely broken my life. Most everyone I knew figured I was done for, that I was beyond hope, yet God miraculously changed my life by setting me free from that affliction and putting me on a new path. I had seen firsthand God's power in action. I knew that God was more than able to keep His promises on helping men and women find real freedom from their addictions.

I also knew that his statement, if true, was an indictment against God. If you followed his train of thought, you could only conclude that God is too weak and powerless to help someone confronted by serious issues. In reality, although unintentional, he was saying that God could only help someone with minor issues, someone who is good, and someone in need of only a little tweaking around the edges.

My first ministry experience working with addicts had mixed results. I saw some spectacular transformations, but mostly the men and women I worked with fell back into their addictions. I found the whole experience very confusing. It seemed to contradict all my education and training related to Gospel ministry. Maybe my friend was right.

My other friends tried to comfort me by reminding me that I should not worry about results. They believed that God was more interested in my faithfulness, rather than the results of my efforts. They intended to help me come to grips with failure. Because they cared about me, they did not want the relapses of men and women in my programs to discourage me beyond repair. If I were still an addict, their words would have brought me nothing but pessimism and grief.

How could I settle for excuses when so many men and women, along with their families, were being destroyed by addiction? I knew that I could never rest until I solved this mystery.

Fortunately, that was only the beginning of my journey. My well-intentioned friend was wrong. Over the years, I have learned that God is indeed stronger than addiction. It took me many years to flesh it out, to develop a program that works. This book is the result of experimentation, trial and error, study and prayer, and personal interaction with thousands of men and women trapped in addiction.

Perhaps you have been asking God to rescue you from substance abuse and set your life on a new path. Twenty-seven years ago, maybe even before you prayed that prayer, God set in motion a series of events that eventually led you to this book. Now the question for you is this: Do you still want God to set you free from addiction?

Your answer to this question will decide your future. Just like me, you must refuse to embrace your current condition, to remain a prisoner of a lifestyle that can only produce destruction, ruin, and pain. Instead, you must embrace God and allow Him to help you finally defeat addiction.

In one sense, I created the program outlined in this book to help me. Even after my addiction lost its influence over my life, character flaws and ingrained habits learned during those addictive years still plagued me. This program has helped me to live life on a higher level. It has changed me.

That does not mean I have arrived or reached a state of perfection. I still struggle with certain areas of life.

I am still growing and developing as a person. I have learned that growth is a lifelong process that makes your life more interesting and meaningful. It also keeps you from slipping back into your self-destructive mode.

My journey of helping men and women change has always been bigger than my personal mission to change my life. I learned years ago that a great life is the result of living for something larger than you are. For me, that means helping as many men and women as possible win their battle with addiction. My passion to help you birthed this book. You can win the addiction battle. Start today!

Sign up for a free workbook for
Winning the Addiction Battle

www.winningtheaddictionbattle.com

Recovery: Just Don't Do it for Yourself

Of all the mess and junk proclaimed by the recovery industry, "just getting sober for you" is one of the biggest myths taught as gospel. They say, "Don't do it for anyone else. Do it for yourself." In other words, sobriety is all about you.

They teach this "fact" with all sincerity and compassion. However, just because the people teaching it are sincere, that does not make it correct. Countless people are sincerely wrong about many things.

When it comes to your life, especially something as important as overcoming your addiction, you need to know the truth. One of the reasons so many people continue to relapse is because they buy into all the false narratives that are part of the current recovery folklore.

Of course, improving your life and getting sober has personal value. One of the primary reasons you go into recovery is to improve the quality of your life and restore personal happiness. That is a given. What I am trying to say is that your welfare is not a big enough incentive to propel you to sobriety. While in your addiction, you self-destructed by focusing on meeting your needs and desires at the expense of your health, reputation, dreams, goals, and personal relationships.

Addiction is an extreme form of self-absorption. When trapped in this nightmare, your entire focus is on satisfying your needs and wants. Look where it got you. Self-centeredness will leave you unsatisfied and deluded about the real meaning of your life. If focusing on yourself were a big enough reason to get clean and sober, you would have already done it.

When your focus is on something larger than your needs, you have a reason to hang tough and not quit when temptation and weakness threaten to engulf you. You need to live your life on a higher plane than just personal gratification.

Addiction is all about adjusting expectations to meet the realities associated with a declining lifestyle. According to conventional wisdom, a person will never embrace change without first hitting bottom. Unfortunately, "bottom" is a loosely defined term that always changes with each new disaster. Each time you relapse, your "bottom" gets deeper. I have seen addicts:

- Eat leftover food out of dumpsters.
- Sleep on sidewalks, in abandon buildings, alleys, and flophouses.
- Choose addiction over employment.
- Commit crimes to satisfy their cravings.
- Manipulate family and friends.
- Trade their children's Christmas and birthday presents for drugs.

I also know from personal experience the depth a person will sink to for them to satisfy personal longings. When addiction ruled my life:

- I sold a valuable car for seventy-five dollars so that I could party.
- I maxed out my mother's credit card.
- I lost jobs because I did not show up for work.
- I spent rent money on alcohol.
- I sold my furniture so I could get drunk.
- I borrowed money from family and friends and never paid them back.
- I broke trust with everyone.

During my addiction, relapse was my middle name. No matter how long I stayed sober, I eventually would find a reason to go out and get drunk. No excuse was too small.

Self-focus has only brought you heartache and pain. It was the driving force behind your addiction. Get your mind off yourself and all your problems. They will only depress you and cause you to relapse. You need to change your focus.

Focus on Relationships

In one sense, addiction is a lonely lifestyle. Although you may have friends, most of them suffer from the same addictions as you do. From experience, you know they will abandon you as soon as they no longer find you useful.

Relationships can be another form of self-focus. When this happens, you use family and friends to meet your needs and accomplish your goals. These types of relationships are another byproduct of your addiction, another form of using. Relationships that only exist for your satisfaction, to meet just your needs, are fleeting and end when you no longer consider that person useful.

I can understand why you might believe that relationships are all about you. It is one of the dominant views in our culture. We are told to abandon relationships that fail to help us achieve our goals, make us feel good about ourselves, or add some value to our lives.

When you unconditionally invest in someone else's life without the expectation of repayment, you take your focus off you and onto meeting the needs of that person. Your goal is to enrich their life, to help them succeed and mature, both emotionally and spiritually.

When you focus just on meeting your needs, you never grow beyond yourself. You limit yourself. Your growth as a person never reaches beyond your insights, wisdom, and experiences. Zig Ziglar, the late, great motivational speaker, and human being, said,

[1]*"You can have everything in life you want if you will just help enough other people get what they want."*

"Help other people" is not some trick or another form of manipulation. You do not calculate the benefit each of your relationships might bring you. You just stay on your mission of adding value to the lives of other people and not worry about how they might help you. Over time, you will see, in very concrete ways, how your service to others has helped change your life.

Focus On Changing the World

One of the things I love about young people is their focus on doing something that will change the world. Their emphasis is more than just donating money and goods. They want to be personally involved in making a difference in the world.

If you want to make a difference in your life, focus on changing someone's world. Here are some suggestions:

- Get involved in a local soup kitchen or food pantry.
- Volunteer at a nursing home.
- Help sort donated clothing and goods.
- Mentor a child or teenager.
- Get involved in an after-school program.
- Help another addict get clean and sober.
- Volunteer at your church.
- Help someone in need.

You have spent enough of your life using people and institutions to advance your personal agenda. If it were not for some of these organizations and individuals, you might be dead today. Someone or some group helped you in your hour of need. Giving back is putting feet to your gratitude.

At this point in your life, you might wonder why you should be grateful for anything. After all, to be grateful, you need

---

[11] "Ziglar Inc - Personal Development Training, Sales Coaching – Plano, Texas."*Ziglar Inc.* N.p., n.d. Web. 21 Mar. 2016.

something good to happen in your life. Getting involved in a cause bigger than you will expand your horizons and help you discover just how fortunate you are. You will grow, mature, and get stronger. Your involvement with others will change you for the better. Focus on changing the world.

Focus on God

Even in your darkest hour, God never abandoned you. He has always had plans for you that are bigger than your addiction, defeats, and disappointments. He loves you in spite of yourself.

Think about some of your worst experiences in life. Maybe God was there, and you just did not realize it.

- An overdose or alcohol poisoning did not kill you. You lived.
- You bought drugs from dangerous people. You are still alive.
- You had a terrible car wreck. You are still here.
- You drove your car or motorcycle while under the influence. You should be amazed that you are still alive.
- You had an experience that you thought would be the end of you. It was not.

Maybe God brought you through those experiences. How else do you explain your miraculous survival despite all the horrible things you experienced while living life as an addict?

Most people have a tendency to become like the object or individual of their focus. Like so many other men and women, when your focus was on addiction, as difficult as it may be to admit, you eventually took on the persona and attitudes of an addict.

If you begin to focus on God, your life and personality become more like him with each passing day. By doing so, you decrease the chances of relapsing back into your old lifestyle.

Begin your focus on God by going to church next Sunday. Although private spirituality is important for a deeper connection with God, it usually is unsustainable without the support of other like-minded individuals. Look for a church that gives you opportunities for personal growth and service to others. Do not reduce your faith to a spectator sport.

Action Steps

If you want to overcome addiction, you cannot have the same attitudes and focuses you had as an addict. Self-focus is the same emphasis you had when trapped in your addiction. Life is not just about meeting your needs. It is so much bigger than that.

No matter where you are in your recovery journey, you need to take these action steps to be successful at living your life:

- Examine all of your relationships by answering the following questions:
    1. What have you done lately to add value to your friends' lives?
    2. Are you encouraging them?
    3. Are you a good listener?
    4. Are you available when they need you?

- Find a cause, ministry, or charity that you can help. Then start volunteering.

- Reconnect with God.
    1. Find a church that will let you get involved. Go to a Bible study or church meeting with a friend.
    2. Begin having daily devotions.
    3. Meet with someone in leadership at the church.
    4. Make sure you attend church this coming Sunday.

As long as your primary focus is on yourself, you are reducing your chances of getting or staying clean and sober. Do not use the same methods that kept you trapped in your addiction. Your life is too important to waste in that way. Live a big life, a life that counts and matters.

Sign up for a free workbook for
Winning the Addiction Battle
www.winningtheaddictionbattle.com

Part One: The Road to Recovery

Have you finally admitted that addiction got the best of you? Perhaps in the past, you tried to quit but eventually relapsed, slipping back into a pit that seemed impossible to escape.

What has your addiction cost you?

- Your job and livelihood
- Your family
- Your health
- Your home
- Your self-respect
- Your future
- Your driver's license

As I told you before, I have been working for twenty-seven years with men and women who are just like you—same problems, addictions, difficulties, and frustrations. Before meeting them, the most difficult person I had ever worked with was me. My addiction to alcohol had completely shattered my life. I lost everything. Fortunately, that was not the final chapter of my life.

Instead of deserting me, God gave me back everything I had squandered and more. He can do the same for you. For that to occur, I had to:

1. I had to admit that I was the real problem in my life, no one else, just me. In other words, I had to accept full responsibility for my actions and the consequences that resulted from them. Most people never get beyond the blame game and remain trapped in their addiction. I hope you are not most people.
2. I had to surrender my life to Christ, not some unknown, nameless higher power. We will talk more about that in a few pages.

3. I had to get involved with other men and women who were traveling the same road as I was. I started going to church. I got involved in small groups so that I could develop deeper, more lasting relationships with others. Not everyone in the small group was battling addiction. However, all of us were struggling to go deeper with God and surrender more of our lives to Him.
4. I had to develop a disciplined, daily devotional plan to help me in my walk with God. More than anything else, I needed his help to keep me from relapsing.
5. I started meeting with other men and women who were experiencing the same struggles with addiction as I was.

If you are like most people, admitting anything unpleasant about your motives, habits, or personality is something you try to avoid. Facing the truth implies taking personal responsibility for the results of your actions. It can make you feel ashamed or embarrassed. Rather than facing the truth, it is easier to place blame on other people or events.

Nevertheless, if you want to win your battle with addiction, you must come to grips with some very unpleasant facts about you. If you do not, you are destined to a life of relapse and self-destruction. Instead of winning the addiction battle, addiction will beat you. It will crush you.

Your response to the next three chapters will determine your fate. You will not like everything you read. It may make you uncomfortable.

The question for you is this: Are you willing to trade the comfort of your addiction for the discomfort of knowing the truth about you?

As you read these chapters, ask God to help you know the truth about you. As difficult as this may be, identifying the actions and attitudes that led to your addiction will result in a huge payoff for you as you progress in your journey. If you do not know the truth about you, you condemn yourself to live a lie.

The purpose of this book is to help you win the addiction battle. I am not trying to make you feel better about your past actions. I am trying to help you overcome your addiction so that you can live a great life. It starts with the truth. It starts today.

I want you to succeed.
Today is the first day of the rest of your life.
Make the most of it.

Four Ways Your Addiction Can Ruin Your Life

Addiction to drugs or alcohol is a game changer. It changes everything about your life—you relationships, finances, security, reputation, and future. Unless you beat addiction, wrestle it to the ground and chase it from your life, it will eventually rob you of everything you hold precious and dear.

Often, when imprisoned in your addiction hell, you begin to view your lifestyle as normal, as an acceptable way to live. You only look for an alternative to your current craziness when you face an unsolvable catastrophe. Unfortunately, the longer you live the addiction lifestyle, the more severe the crisis must be to get your attention.

At some point in your life, when you are no longer able to handle your nightmare, your survival will depend on your willingness to face the truth about your circumstances, addiction, and future. Without an honest assessment of your life, you will never escape addiction's stranglehold on you. You must face the truth about you.

Take a few moments, and finish reading this chapter. Think very carefully about the points I am making. The next few minutes have the potential to be life changing for you. How you react to what I am about to say may have a significant impact on your future. If possible, try to have an open mind. Ask God to show you if the things I write are true.

Here are four ways your addiction can destroy your life:

1) **Your addiction can ruin your relationships**.

You probably already know from personal experience that this is true. Most relationships collapse under the weight of addictive behavior. When addiction rules your life, it takes the place of all of the important relationships in your life. Addiction wants you exclusively for itself. It destroys every single vital relationship in your life—your spouse, significant other, kids, parents, siblings, friends, and other relatives.

Your new relationships brought into your life by addiction are conditional and temporary at best. As long as you have money, drugs, and alcohol, a mob of adoring friends is with you every moment. When your stuff runs out, they run out. They leave you to fend for yourself. You find yourself alone, depressed, and maybe even suicidal.

The people who care about you mostly gave up trying to help you. You have hurt and disappointed them too many times. They may still love you and care about what happens to you, but they cannot take the pain anymore. Your pattern with them is disillusionment and sorrow, often punctured with intense feelings of betrayal. You have become like a deadly poison to them, someone to avoid at all cost.

No man or woman without friends and significant relationships is truly rich. Profound and abiding relationships are the true measure of a person's life.

If addiction has not yet wrecked all of your valuable relationships, it will. Just give it time. Addiction will not suffer long any competition for its affections. In reality, addiction is not your friend; it is your enemy. It cuts the heart out of your life. Without your family and friends, you are alone. In essence, you just exist, almost like a zombie. You are condemned to live life as a member of the walking dead, alive in name only.

Warning: Do not let addiction ruin your life by robbing you of your relationships.

2) **Your addiction will ruin your finances**.

It does not matter what your financial position is when your addiction begins to take over your life. Eventually, it will gain control of your finances. It wants to control every aspect of your life.

When I lived in San Francisco, we met a young homeless man who had spent the night sleeping in an alley, using a filthy garbage bag to keep warm. He was addicted to crack-cocaine. This young man came from a well-known, wealthy family. You have probably heard of them. His family had set up for him a trust fund that mailed him a check twice a year. Despite all his wealth, crack owned him and his finances.

Some people can live as functional addicts. Unfortunately, over time, their façade of respectability begins to break down as their addictive behavior gains increasing control over their lives. Addiction is never a winning proposition.

Here are some ways your addiction can ruin your finances:

- Your addiction consumes your money. You cannot pay your bills.
- Your addiction makes you undependable at work. You eventually lose your job.
- Your addiction causes you to lose your license. You cannot drive.
- Your financial difficulties cause strife between you and your lenders. You cannot pay them back.
- You begin to steal money out of your spouse's wallet or purse. He or she kicks you out, hoping you will come to your senses.
- You sleep on a couch at a friend's house. Eventually, you run out of friends.
- Maybe you steal, shoplift, or embezzle money. It only gets worse.

I cannot believe you want to see your finances ruined. Your financial collapse will undermine your health, your security, your relationships, and your future. Do you believe that your addiction is worth losing everything you possess? Do you want to live in misery the rest of your life?

Warning: Do not let addiction ruin your life by reducing you to poverty.

3) Your addiction will ruin your reputation.

If you are not yet acquainted with the criminal justice system, it is only a matter of time before it becomes a significant part of your life. DUIs, possession, petty theft, shoplifting, public drunkenness, and other crimes are part of the addictive lifestyle. Your addiction will make you do things and go places you never dreamed possible before you began your present journey.

Not only will you break the law to satisfy your addiction, but you will also alienate your friends, family, and business acquaintances by your actions and behavior. Some will even look down on you with contempt. Here is a partial list of socially unacceptable behaviors that will become descriptive of you if you do not change your way of life:

- You will get angry with people for not believing your lies.
- You will master the art of deceitful manipulation.
- You will become unreliable, someone who cannot be trusted to take care of even basic responsibilities.
- You will neglect your job and your family.
- Your addictive behavior will embarrass your friends and loved ones.
- You will eventually neglect your appearance and hygiene.
- Your behavior will cause people not to trust you.

Your reputation will determine the value of your relationships, business connections, and future opportunities. Without a solid reputation, it will be hard to find someone willing to take a chance on you, to help you succeed at life. When you ruin your reputation, you wreck your future.

Warning: Do not let your addiction rob you of your future by ruining your reputation.

4) Your addiction can ruin your health.

Without your health, the quality of your life is severely impaired. I have seen young, once healthy men and women, crippled by health issues that never should have happened. Tragically, their addiction caused them to neglect proper heath precautions and behaviors.

My brother died young because of his addiction to alcohol. He was a brilliant software engineer who had the world at his feet. One day his neighbors found him face down in the gutter in front of his big house in Florida. He lost his sight, his ability to walk, and both his short-term and long-term memory.

His body broke down because he failed to eat while he was drinking. He depleted the vitamins in his body, causing the issues I just described. Eventually, he regained his sight, long-term memory, and ability to walk. Since he never regained his short-term memory, he was unable to work ever again. Several months before he died, I remember him standing in front of the toilet and asking me to explain to him what he needed to do to relieve himself. He could not remember what to do. He was only fifty-three when he died. It did not have to happen.

Your addiction will take your health from you. It will also ruin your teeth and your wonderful smile. Do you want that to happen? Was that the plan for your life? Although the body can be very resilient, it will ultimately succumb to your addictive lifestyle.

Warning: Do not let your addiction destroy your health. Do not waste your life.

The four things I have listed for you are not theories or just possibilities. They will certainly pay you a visit if you continue to let addiction control your life. Here is what you need to do:

- Make a decision today to do whatever it takes to defeat your addiction.
- If you relapse, quit crying. Get back on your feet, and try again. Eventually, you will succeed.
- Get help. You cannot do it alone.
- Ask God to help you. He has a bigger plan for you than addiction.

The decisions you make today determine what kind of life you will live. What decision will you make about your addiction?

Will you choose ruin or success?

Sign Up for Free Materials to
Help you Win the Addiction Battle

www.winningtheaddictionbattle.com

Mindsets that Cause You to Relapse

One of the primary reasons addicts are unable to make changes in their lives is the belief that there is no cure for addiction. Addiction, according to this view, is genetic, predisposing an individual to a life of self-destruction and pain. So often, the person trapped in addiction, frustrated by frequent relapses, surrenders to failure, believing that their "disease" prevents them from ever living a normal life. Why go through the struggle of getting clean since the results are always the same?

I will never forget a young woman I met named Gladys. A former prostitute who had found redemption through our ministry introduced me to Gladys. Gladys was several months pregnant, addicted to heroin, and, because of her addiction, forced to prostitute her body to support her habit. According to society, she was a three-time loser, a wasted life, a leech upon her community.

Gladys's first week with us was tough. As you probably already know, it is not a pleasant sight to watch someone detox from heroin; yet for her to get to the other side of addiction, she had to walk through the suffering entailed in rooting the addiction from her body. After a week or so, she began to regain her strength.

After Gladys had been with us for several weeks, she started talking to some of the other women she knew from the streets. All of them were prostitutes with horrible addiction problems. Since she did not know how to explain clearly the recent changes in her life, she brought them to me. Each time she said, "Tell them what you said to me." It was exciting to see what God was doing in her life.

One day, five of the most beautiful children you have ever seen showed up on the front steps of the mission. "Is my mommy here?" they asked. They were looking for Gladys. When she came outside, the children were overjoyed to see her. "Mommy! Mommy!" they cried. "We are so happy to see you. We miss you,

Mommy. We love you, Mommy." It warmed my heart to watch this emotional reunion.

Gladys's mother was raising her children. Like most addicts, Gladys was unable to raise her children; instead of choosing her kids, she chose heroin.

I noticed one of her little girls in particular. The other kids led her around by her hand. She was blind, the result of Gladys's heroin use during the pregnancy. Of all the children, she seemed to be the one who loved her mom the most. Tears welled up in my eyes as I watched this little blind child, a victim of her mother's irresponsibility.

Several days later, I returned to the mission after running a few errands. When I walked through the door, one of the men in my program told me that Gladys had disappeared. They suspected she had gone to one of the local parks several blocks away. This park was not like the parks most people take their kids to on a Sunday afternoon. It was notorious for drug dealing, gang activity, and prostitution. Broken wine bottles and empty syringes littered the ground. It was a place of darkness and death.

Immediately, I ran out of the mission and headed straight for the park. I found Gladys sitting on the ground, leaning up against a tree. Her eyes were rolling back in her head, and a fresh needle puncture on her arm dripped tiny droplets of blood, a sure sign that she had just injected heroin into her vein. She looked up at me and began to cry. "I tried, Rev. I tried, but this is what I am. I cannot change. It's too hard."

Are you like Gladys? Do you view your shortcomings, destructive habits, and addiction as incurable diseases, beyond the reach of all your efforts to overcome them? Have your constant struggles to transform your character often flopped, teaching you to give up on change, surrender to failure, and settle on remaining an addict for the rest of your life?

Do you believe your personality and character are unchangeable, resistant to all your efforts to become someone more decent and stable? Maybe you simply do not believe you can change. So why try?

If you try to deal with your problem using typical therapeutic methods, your addiction will act like a disease that has no cure. You are stuck with it for the rest of your life.

The good news is, God is stronger than your addiction and can help you conquer it for the last time.

Do not fall into the false belief that you were born to be an addict. God means for you to live a life that excludes addiction. God is more than capable of permanently reversing your condition and addictive lifestyle. Do not fail because you think addiction is your destiny. It is not!

You Fail Because You Are Afraid to Trust God

Sometimes God's methods are difficult to love. He seems willing to employ whatever method he deems necessary to produce a positive change in your life. Occasionally his methods produce sorrow, suffering, and pain. Perhaps you are afraid that his way of improving you will feel more like punishment than help.

Your fear of God's plans can become an obstacle that prevents real and lasting personal change from taking place. Like most people, you want to substitute quick and easy fixes, methods that rarely produce permanent change, in place of the tried and trusted methods of God.

However, when you continue to trust God in your challenging experiences, you are proclaiming that God's plans are the better way. The pain and suffering that he allows into your life produce fruit that could not be harvested using lesser means. If you are interested in personal change, you need to accept that God is in the best position to determine what is necessary for that change to take place.

Do not let your fear of God prevent you from trusting him for deliverance from your addiction. Once you are free from substance abuse and experiencing your new life, you will eventually realize that trusting God was the smartest thing you ever did.

"Cast all your anxiety on him because he cares for you."
I Peter 5:7 (NIV)

You Fail Because You Are Impatient for Results

Our modern conveniences have taught us to expect immediate gratification and satisfaction in all areas of life. We have learned to be anxious for results and easily frustrated by any obstacle that slows our efforts to achieve goals and obtain rewards. We end up complaining about download speeds, cooking times, computer startup times, and response times. The list of frustrations is almost endless.

Most self-help books have titles that speak to this frustration. They promise quick and efficient methods for making changes in your life. Unfortunately, many self-help books become an additional source of frustration due to their unfulfilled promises of swift change.

Because you have no staying power or patience for change, you often give up and quit. You conclude that it must not be a worthwhile endeavor since the results are so slow in occurring. Your hurriedness causes you to settle for less than what you could become. You end up missing relationships and experiences that could add real value and depth to your life.

Patience is the key to virtue and freedom. So often, people quit right when they are on the verge of a breakthrough that will change everything. They never recognize exactly how close they came to succeeding.

In your journey to beat addiction and change your life, I urge you not to quit. Despite all outward appearances, your victory over addiction is closer than you think.

In Galatians 6:9 (ESV), we read,

"And let us not grow weary of doing good, for in due season we will reap, if we do not give up."

You Fail Because You Try to Do It in Your Strength

If you could have changed using your power, you probably would not be reading this book. You would have already beaten your addiction. Even though you may have devoted years of vigorous effort trying to make significant changes in your life, you have seen little in the way of results.

Because you do not want to be a hypocrite, you have lowered your standards or your definition of success to a level you can attain using your strength. If you are already a Christian, you might have concluded: "After all, I'm saved by faith, not by works. God will forgive me no matter what I do."

Your personal strength and willpower can only go so far on changing deep-seated habits and character issues. God is the only one who can transform you by creating the image of Christ in your life. Your strength will never suffice. As a matter of fact, in II Corinthians 12:8-9 (ESV), the Apostle Paul emphatically states,

"Three times I pleaded with the Lord about this, that it should leave me. But he said to me, 'My grace is sufficient for you, for my power is made perfect in weakness.' Therefore I will boast all the more gladly of my weaknesses, so that the power of Christ may rest upon me."

God can do His best work in your life when you reach the end of your strength. When you recognize that you are helpless to make a major makeover in your life using your resources and abilities, you will have happily reached the starting point for God's power to step in and begin the process of changing your life. Only God's strength is sufficient for changing the deep-rooted flaws in your character and habits.

The outer limits of human strength are the starting point for God's power.

What has your personal experience with recovery taught you? Have you finally learned that your skills and talents are incapable of setting you free from addiction? If you have reached this point in your life, you are now in an enviable position. How exciting for you! Your incredible adventure is about to begin.

You Fail Because You Try to Do It Alone

Think about our heritage. Stories of rugged individuals, lonely prophets in the wilderness, and courageous men and women standing alone against injustice and persecution fill our history books. They have become our models, inspiring us to be the captains of our ships and the masters of our destinies.

On occasion, events require solitary effort, one man or woman against the whole world. Even so, those examples are not the norm. When God created men and women, he never intended for them to be alone. When Adam was alone in the garden, God stated that He created Eve so that Adam would not be alone.

God uses your relationships with other people to bring change into your life. Interaction with others sharpens, corrects, and enables personal growth; relationships provide you with insights and support that help you succeed beyond what you could have achieved by yourself.

Relationships also encourage you; they help you persevere when you run out of strength and are on the verge of relapsing back into the pit of hell. Friendships and mentors are essential for living a life beyond addiction. They bring you joy and contentment. They make the struggle to get clean worth the effort.

You Fail Because You Lack Discipline

Most of you abhor the very thought of anything that might possible squelch the free-flow of spontaneity in your life. You believe structure and discipline smack too much of legalism, a crushing burden that inhibits the unfettered growth of your individuality and progress.

For you to accomplish anything of significance in life, structure and discipline are required. Athletes, soldiers, artists, health professionals, and many others succeed in life because they are willing to practice discipline in their lives, to pay the price and make personal sacrifices to reach their goals. In I Timothy 4:7 (ESV) we read, "... train yourself for godliness ...." Godliness, according to the Scriptures, requires training, just as athletic success is the culmination of a disciplined training schedule.

If you want to change, then according to the Bible, you must have a plan. Without a plan, you have a plan for failure. One of the primary reasons you fail to change is because you lack the discipline essential for change.

Conclusion

Faulty mindsets can only produce flawed results. It is important to know the truth, think the right thoughts, and do the right things. In your battle with addiction, truth unconnected to God will continue to wreck your life and destroy your future. Only God's truth will rescue you from yourself and give you a life that is worth living.

How Relapse and Failure Can Help You

Relapse and failure can be the catalysts that assist you in defeating addiction and changing your life.

Addiction can be a tough war to win. For many, relapse and failure pave the path to sobriety. In your battle to change your life, you will experience some heartbreaking setbacks. You will sometimes fail.

When you relapse or fail, you will be tempted to wallow in your failure and guilt, to replay the incident repeatedly in your mind, to let it destroy you. You will experience lots of frustration and sorrow. You will not be able to think straight. You will feel hopeless, unable to imagine life without drugs or alcohol.

Even worse, you might refuse to admit responsibility for your condition and resort to blaming other people, genetics, or your background for your relapse or failure. Instead of using failure as a tool to advance your life, you sentence yourself to a life of bitterness, misery, and constant relapse.

I have never met a person who had not failed at something in life. All of us fail. For some, failure is a stopover on the way to success. They view failure as a teaching moment, an educational tool that prepares them to take life to another level.

Others learn the wrong lessons from failure, muddying their futures and preventing them from enjoying the fruit of a meaningful life.

These false lessons can teach you:

- Not to trust others because they might hurt you
- Never take a risk because you might fail
- To be careful about trying something new because it might disappoint you
- To quit believing that your dreams are possible

- That success is only for other people
- That you will always be an addict

Seeing failure as an opportunity instead of a final destination does not diminish its devastating emotional impact or lessen its consequences in your life. Your failure can cause real emotional pain and guilt. It may also ruin your finances, destroy your most significant relationships, and seriously frustrate your efforts to achieve your goals. Sometimes failure's impact on your life can take years to turn around.

I listen to many podcasts about entrepreneurship. Most of the people on the podcasts are young and successful. Many of them endured a great many difficulties to succeed. One of the most oft-quoted sayings I hear is, "Fail early and fail often." Others say, "Fail your way to success."

I understand the truth they are trying to teach. The fear of failure is a paralyzing condition that infects most of humanity. It prevents most people from achieving success and sentences significant portions of them to a life of dullness and mediocrity. It is a dream-killer.

For those of you who have experienced real failure, perhaps even more than once, failure produced distressing consequences in your life. It made you feel ugly inside, like a loser who can never win. You felt:

- You had let down people who trusted you
- Guilt for making bad decisions
- Hopeless about your future
- Depressed
- Confused

You also experienced real, awful consequences because of failure:

- A mountain of debt
- Unrepairable broken relationships
- Financial destruction

- A loss of employment

Addiction can bring you additional, distressing penalties:

- Felony convictions
- Disease
- Homelessness
- Prison
- Loss of your driver's license
- Death

I do not think failure should be a goal or something you should desire just because it can help you discover important truths about yourself and the pathway to success. If you can avoid taking the wrong path, do not take it. It is not necessary to learn everything the hard way.

Still, what do you do once you have failed? How can it help you? What can you learn from it?

I am writing this chapter for men and women who have already failed, hit bottom, and wrecked important parts of their lives.

Several years ago, one of the men in one of my residential programs approached me with a question. He asked, "Who will ever hire me? I have five felony convictions. What's the use of even trying to get clean?"

I responded: "There are very few business owners who will hire you with five felony convictions. Your only option is to start your own business." I knew that someone had to tell him the truth. Otherwise, he would waste too much of his life living in a fantasyland.

In reality, he only had two choices. He could let his past determine his future by continuing to live like a convicted felon without any options. On the other hand, he could learn from his past actions and develop a new plan for his life based on what he had learned from his previous mistakes.

The second option requires an answer to the following questions: What lessons can you learn from your past actions that will help you change your future? What does your past teach you about yourself? If you learn from your past, you are not fated to repeat it.

The unfortunate truth about addiction, alcohol, or drugs is that most people have to experience a great deal of emotional pain before even seeing the need to make necessary changes in their lives. Even when they make changes, they hardly ever stick to their plan and eventually relapse back into their former life. They waste valuable lessons their pain and loss could have taught them. Unfortunately, their next relapse experience is usually even more painful. Over time, the experiences get even more intense and consequential.

"Fail early and fail often" may be a great philosophy for the business sector, perhaps even the nonprofit sector, but it is not a wise philosophy for your life. When you chose addiction, on purpose or by your actions, you chose disaster. Without some dramatic intervention, you will create a personal hell for yourself that may hold you captive for many years. For the person trapped in addiction, failure rarely leads to success. It leads to more failure and personal destruction.

Most people continue to fail and relapse because they refuse to learn valuable lessons from previous failures.

Many of you reading this book have a long history of relapse and failure. Deep down, although you would never publically admit it, you believe you are a failure, a loser, someone who never wins. Others of you have family members and friends held captive in the lifestyle of addiction. You want to help them.

Zig Ziglar stated an important truth about failure that you should memorize. He said,

[2]*"Remember that failure is an event, not a person."*

---

[2]"Zig Ziglar Facebook Page." N.p., n.d. Web. 21 Mar. 2016.

You may have made decisions that caused you to fail; your reaction to failure determines whether it is just a temporary experience or a permanent description of who you are as a person. No one is a failure who decides to learn from his or her mistakes and decides to do something about it.

Failure is similar to going to a vocational school to learn a trade. At vocational school, you spend an insignificant amount of your time on theories and abstractions. Your focus is on learning a trade that will pay your bills and give you a comfortable life. In the same way, failure trains you to succeed in life—your job, relationships, responsibilities, etc.

Failure teaches you the truth about you. Dishonesty is a primary character trait of a man or woman gripped by addiction. Deceitfulness may bring you temporary relief from some of your pain. Despite that, in the end, your pain always returns. In its return, it exposes you as the responsible actor for the damage and chaos in your life.

You have spent years trying to convince yourself that you are not liable for your present condition. It is always someone else's fault; you are never to blame. Even when you do take responsibility, you do it primarily as a tool for influencing other people to give you money or something else you need.

If you want to learn from your failure, you must accept personal responsibility for the actions that led to your destruction. If you do not, you condemn yourself to an endless cycle of relapse and failure.

Face the Truth about Yourself

A careful study of the behavior and mindsets that led to your failure will reveal some unpleasant truths that may be difficult for you to swallow. Nevertheless, be relentless in your pursuit of the facts. Whatever remains hidden will resurrect itself at some future date, short-circuiting your recovery and bringing you unnecessary pain and suffering.

Sometimes the truth will be almost too much for you to bear. To minimize your suffering, you will try to justify your failure, to make excuses for your addiction and thereby escape the emotional consequences of knowing the truth.

In our therapeutic society, we have become experts at shifting blame. So many people are deluded into believing, despite all the evidence to the contrary, in the universal goodness of human beings. This belief causes them to look for external reasons or causes to explain their destructive behavior. In one sense, this idea foreshadows the end of personal responsibility.

Even in Christian circles, we try to make ourselves imagine that we are creatures of infinite value. After all, the Creator of the universe sent His Son to die on the cross for us. Surely, Jesus would not die for us if we were worthless junk. For such a sacrifice, it is reasonable to assume there must be something of fundamental worth in each of us, something worthy of his death. Moreover, we continue by saying, "God didn't make junk."

Although I do not wish to call anyone junk, maybe the word is helpful for understanding your condition and God's relationship to you. Junk is a word that knocks down the pretensions that prevent you from acknowledging responsibility for the ugliness and pain in your life.

In one sense, it does not matter what your condition was at your birth. What is important is what you have become, what you are today.

Despite all your efforts to place blame elsewhere for your current predicament, you do know the truth about you. You do know what kind of person you have become. When the Bible says in Romans 3:10 (ESV), "None is righteous, no, not one," you know it is talking about you. You are too smart to lie to yourself forever.

Sometimes your feelings of guilt and worthlessness are too overpowering; they bury all your efforts to maintain a positive attitude. At some point in time, you lost the ability to be encouraged by motivational one-liners and messages. Positive thinking has become a source of discouragement and disappointment. It no longer works.

Truth has a funny way of overwhelming all of your false ideas about you.

I know that the word junk must be an insult to your self-esteem. I do not like it either. If you are like most people, you can admit that you made some mistakes, but junk?

What exactly is junk? Junk is something that can no longer fulfill its purpose. It is useless, without value. Although it may have been valuable at one time, because of wear and tear, abuse, and lack of care, it lost its original worth. Eventually, it ended up in the garbage, at a junk yard, or in a dumpsite littered with other junk.

Then along comes the junk collector who sees potential value in the object. The junk collector restores the value of the junk and returns it to usefulness. It is no longer junk.

The Bible has a definite view about human goodness. Please read these verses:

"We're all sin-infected, sin-contaminated. Our best efforts are grease-stained rags."
Isaiah 64:6 (The Message Bible)

"There's nobody living right, not even one, nobody who knows the score, nobody alert for God. They've all taken the wrong turn; they've all wandered down blind alleys. No one's living right; I can't find a single one."
Romans 3:9-12 (The Message Bible)

"I realize that I don't have what it takes. I can will it, but I can't do it. I decide to do good, but I don't really do it; I decide not to do bad, but then I do it anyway. My decisions, such as they are, don't result in actions. Something has gone wrong deep within me and gets the better of me every time."
Romans 7:18 (The Message Bible)

These are hard words. Fortunately, these Bible verses just set the stage for the good news. The Apostle Paul spells out this great news by saying,

> "Here's a word you can take to heart and depend on: Jesus Christ came into the world to save sinners. I'm proof—Public Sinner Number One—of someone who could never have made it apart from sheer mercy. And now he shows me off—evidence of his endless patience—to those who are right on the edge of trusting him forever."
> I Timothy 1:15-16 (The Message Bible)

I am so grateful that our God is a junk collector. We are the discarded junk. God recycles junk into something useful and productive. This truth sets us free. We are free because this truth tells us that God loves us in spite of ourselves. When the whole world proclaims we are worthless junk, we know that our God loved us and gave his life for us. Because of His sacrifice, we do not have to be afraid to admit the truth.

I once knew two men who made their living scrapping junk. Every day they would drive their pickup truck up and down the alleys of the city looking for scraps of discarded metal and unwanted objects set out for the garbage collectors. They would sell the metal at the area scrap yards and the other items at flea markets. They collected discarded junk and used it to pay their rent and feed their families. They were able to turn unwanted junk into something useful and valuable.

God can take the mess you have made of your life and use it to transform your future.

Recognizing the truth about you can be a catalyst for change. Once confronted with the truth about you, you can either ignore the facts or decide that you no longer want to be that kind of person. You choose to change.

If you want to know the truth about you, ask God for help. Why compound your pain by spending years living a lie? After all, how can you begin the process of change without knowing what needs changing? In Psalm 129:33-34 (ESV), we read,

"Search me, O God, and know my heart! Try me and know my thoughts! And see if there be any grievous way in me, and lead me in the way everlasting!"

Facing My Truth

Recently while driving in our car, I looked at my wife and said, "Honey, if I hadn't been such a loser, I never would have met you." As you might imagine, she was not very impressed with my statement. Most people would have interpreted my words as a major putdown, an insinuation that if I had been more successful in life, I could have done better in my choice of a marriage partner.

That is not what I meant at all. Next to my relationship with Jesus, my relationship with my wife is the greatest thing that has ever happened to me. She brings me happiness and joy. My best moments of the day are the moments I spend with her. While I am easily bored with most things in life, she has never been boring to me. To me, she is the most exciting person I have ever met.

In my early thirties, I went back to school to study for the ministry. I had spent the previous ten years trapped in alcohol addiction, depression, and ruin. I blamed everyone but myself for the pain in my life—for the broken relationships, for all the failures, and for my profound sense of alienation and abandonment.

While in school, I obtained a job at the Raleigh Rescue Mission, a place of hope for men and women who had lost their way. Addiction and bad decisions put them in a position of total dependency upon the generosity of strangers for meeting their most basic needs. How could such terrible things happen in a person's life, things so destructive they reduced a person to begging for food, sleeping in alleys and abandoned buildings, wasting meager resources on drugs or alcohol, and destroying every significant relationship that mattered?

Although I wanted to be polite, I finally broke down and asked them how such an awful fate had befallen them. Their explanations were thick with cynicism and anger: "My mother abandoned me." "My father was abusive." "My wife left me." "People hurt me." As I listened to their reasons for their homelessness and addiction, I noticed one common theme woven throughout each of their explanations—someone else was responsible for their predicament.

As they told me their stories, I began to hear my voice in their descriptions of their personal tragedies. I was just like them. I had spent my adult life dodging personal responsibility for the waste in my life. It was always someone else's fault, never my own. I portrayed myself as a victim, as though I bore no responsibility for the wreckage that shadowed my life.

Without realizing it, I had embraced victimhood. For me, it was a place of comfort and security. This place shielded me from the pain of admitting the truth about me: I was a loser. Yes, bad things had happened to me, people had hurt me, but I chose to respond by lashing out and hurting myself and everyone else I knew.

As I learned the truth about me, I whined, "How can God ever use a loser like me? Instead of growing my life, I wasted so much of my time and energy crying in my coffee, blaming others for my difficulties and missing opportunities that would have changed the whole direction of my life. Will anyone ever trust me again?"

After so many years of escape and evasion, of blaming others for my failures, I finally summoned up the courage to take personal responsibility for my actions and their results. As painful as it was, it was the beginning of a new chapter in my life. Without my admission of guilt, I would have remained trapped in a seemingly endless cycle of failure and relapse.

What is so amazing to me is how the power of God's love has transformed my life. He took my rebellion, selfishness, and pain and used it to help me start ministries that are affecting thousands of people each day. What a wondrous God he is! He uses Rebels, losers, and troublemakers to accomplish His will. He does not leave us in a swamp of uselessness. He brings us to a higher level, a place we could not have journeyed to on our own. He uses our past to build us a new future. Once God gets a hold of you, nothing in your life is wasted. He uses it all to accomplish his purpose for you.

It is Time to Admit That You Are the Problem

Over the years, people have told me some unsettling stories about themselves. I have heard graphic tales of adultery, porn addiction, violence, murder, deception, robbery, etc. You name it; I have probably heard about it. But then I've also heard accounts, perhaps even more disturbing because they seem so harmless in comparison, of gossiping that murders reputations, critical attitudes that smother everyone they touch, greed that takes advantage of the misfortune of others, selfishness that destroys relationships, jealousy that wrecks marriages, etc. The list is almost non-ending.

Many of these unhappy tales of personal destruction and failure shared the same storyline: Each person who told me their story, with few exceptions, said that despite the damage she had produced in her life and the lives of others, deep down, she was a decent person. All the misery that surrounded her life was the product of trying circumstances, genetic dispositions, or undeserved abuse from a family member or friend.

Maybe you are finding it too difficult to admit that you are the cause of so much of the pain in your life. You are not alone. Most people cannot accept personal responsibility for their behavior. It is always easier and less painful to affix blame elsewhere.

This practice means that you can never know the truth about yourself, thus spoiling all your attempts to live a life filled with significance and purpose. I bet that sometimes, to evade the real facts about you, you say whatever you need to say to suppress and hide the real details behind your motives and actions. Without facing the truth about you, you will never defeat addiction.

> "... and you will know the truth, and the truth will set you free."
> John 8:32 (ESV)

Your failure or relapse can help you begin a new journey in your life. Here is what the truth can teach you that will help you overthrow addiction and succeed with your life:

- Taking personal responsibility for your actions can help you move beyond the insanity of endlessly repeating the same mistakes.
- When you admit responsibility for your self-destruction, you are then open to learning new behaviors that produce results that are more positive.
- When you finally confess the truth about yourself, you become willing to do whatever it takes to change.
- The ugly truth helps you to rely on God instead of yourself.

You may not be able to change the outward influences that surround you, but you can modify the way you react to those forces. Ultimately, your reactions will determine your future.

Do you believe that your past has ruined your future? If so, stop! God is stronger than your past. He will use it to create a life for you far beyond your comprehension. Do not be afraid to face the truth about you. Learn from your failures. God already knows everything there is to know about you. It does not scare Him.

Part Two: The God Connection

God has a purpose for your life. It never included addiction, self-destruction, jail, or any of the other consequences associated with an addictive lifestyle. Even though you may have lost your way, God can still get you back on the path that leads to your destiny.

You may have given up on yourself, but God has not given up on you. Even now, he is patiently waiting for you to surrender your life to Him. Nothing in your past discourages God from having a relationship with you. In spite of yourself, he has never stopped loving you.

Connecting with God is the most important thing you can do to change your life. Only God has the power to defeat your addiction and help you build a brand-new life. Without that connection, you will quickly discover that your addiction is greater than your ability. No matter how much grit and determination you may have, it is dreadfully inadequate to loosen and eventually vanquish your habit from your life. It is a battle that you cannot win without his help.

Connecting with God will eventually lead you to a life of purpose, contentment, and joy. It will change everything. You will never be the same again.

As I write these words, I am praying for you. I might not know your name, but God does. Your future is in the balance. I pray you will choose wisely.

It All Begins With Christ

The previous chapters have prepared you for the chapter you are about to read. Read it carefully. This chapter is your turning point from addiction to a brand-new life.

Important Truths in this Chapter

- If you want God to help you defeat addiction, you must first surrender your life to Christ.
- God is more powerful than your addiction or past failures.
- In God's hands, your past is not wasted. He uses it to create your future.
- God loves you even when you have made a mess out of your life.
- You do not have to be perfect.
- God changes you through your relationship with him.

There has to be a starting point, the beginning of a journey, the first step. You cannot take the first step until you have decided where you want to go. If you choose to become a doctor, then your first step is your education. If your ambition is to become a welder, then you have to learn how to weld. Your goal, dream, or objective will determine how you begin your journey.

If you want to change your life, become different from who and what you are today, get the better of addiction and spend eternity with God, then you start with Christ. Life change, moral reform, and character rehabilitation are mostly spiritual endeavors rooted in a committed relationship with God. You can use multiple methods to achieve and grow that relationship–church attendance, Christian television, Bible reading, etc.; but it cannot even begin to become a reality unless you take the first step of surrendering your life to Christ.

Why Surrender to Christ?

Why do you have to surrender your life to Christ? Why not just become a little religious and let God do the rest. Unfortunately, a part-time religion will never be sufficient for a full-time life. If you want a successful marriage, try telling your spouse that you only want to be married part-time.

So why begin with Christ? Why not just go straight to God and let him work his magic on you? Tragically, going straight to God is impossible because you, like all other men and women, have a significant problem that hinders all your efforts to connect with God. That problem is your sin. Your sin has disconnected you from God. In your life, that disconnection revealed itself through the chaos of your addiction.

God Can Use You Despite Your Personal Failures

In my ministry to the homeless, I have seen how addiction can cause a man or woman to damage their whole life, wreck their most significant relationships, and destroy any safety net that may have prevented their downfall. Then again, self-destruction is not limited to the inner city or the homeless. I have seen addiction wreck the lives of executives and CEOs, men and women in the trades, politicians, models, ministers, the wealthy, and countless other people.

Fortunately, I have seen God take these same, seemingly impossible, people with their unbearable situations and use them to accomplish something great.

Often when faced with your failures, you feel helpless—condemned to frustration and hopelessness, as though your particular hole is too deep for you to escape. You feel that your weakness has made you useless and unproductive.

As I study the Bible, I do not see your failures and shortcomings frightening God. The sight of you face down in the dirt, struggling to breathe, positive that your future is over, does not frighten God. Do you think God is afraid, fearful that his power is too weak for your problems? Do you believe that your condition or situation is so unique that God has no plan for fixing or using it to produce something great in your life? When God appears, he takes your wasted life and transforms it into something productive and useful, a portrait of Christ, a life filled to the brim with meaning and significance.

The Bible is full of stories of men and women who experienced disastrous failures in their lives; yet because of God's mercy, his love of using fragile and broken vessels, they were able to accomplish great things for God's kingdom.

God Uses Your Past to Transform Your Future

When you surrender your life to Christ, God does not automatically reset your life, pushing you forward as though you are a person without a past, an empty slate. No, he does something even stronger than that. He uses the pieces of your life, your hurts, pains, successes, failures, depression, feelings of abandonment and rejection, much like a jigsaw puzzle, and forms a new person in you, a person with potential and a future.

When you invite Christ into your life, nothing from your past is wasted. He uses it all to make you into something new and beautiful.

I initially surrendered my life to Christ shortly after my twenty-first birthday. Sensing that God had His hand on me for full-time service, I enrolled at a Christian college to study for the ministry. While at college, members of the philosophy department invited me to major in that discipline. Many of my professors encouraged me to persevere in my studies. They believed that my calling in life was to become a seminary or college professor.

I never became a seminary professor. I reverted to my old life as a drunk and completely trashed my life. I spent almost six years lost in this wilderness before regaining my sanity.

It is impossible for me to know what my life might have become if I had not lost my way. I am sure that it was never God's will for me to self-destruct, to hurt so many others and myself. However, I chose that path, one action and response at a time. I am so grateful that God did not throw me on the garbage heap, leaving me to deteriorate into an old, bitter person who was angry at the world and filled with regret and sorrow.

Instead of abandoning me, God has used my broken life to bring blessings and hope to many others. If I had not lost my way, I never would have met my wife; I would never have started the missions that have served over fifteen million hot meals to the homeless and needy and influenced the lives of thousands. I would never have adopted our kids and rescued them from poverty and danger or lived a life filled with so much adventure and excitement.

I do know this: God still has a plan for you. While you have breath, he believes in you, has plans to prosper you and not hurt you, and wants to use you for something great. He is waiting for you to come to the end of your struggling and floundering and fling yourself into his arms of compassion and strength.

God Loves You in Spite of Yourself

Your value as an individual does not depend on something good inside of you; no, your value is based on who God is and his love for you. His love for you is not dependent on perfect behavior, mighty deeds, or incredible sacrifice. It is central to his very nature. The essence of God is love. He automatically loves you because love is who he is.

This truth is not just something that theologians have discovered. In Romans 5:8 (ESV) we read,

"But God shows his love for us in that while we were still sinners, Christ died for us."

God proved His love for you by what He did on the cross. The very Creator of the universe gave up his throne, surrendered himself to the power of brutal men, and died. However, it was not the death of a helpless victim, powerless to rescue himself from his accusers. No, it was the death of the One who holds the power of life and death in his hands. He willingly chose to renounce it for the sake of his love for you and me.

Why did he do it? Why did he lay down His life? In Romans 6:23 (ESV) we read, "For the wages of sin is death, but the free gift of God is eternal life in Christ Jesus our Lord."

He did it to give you another chance at life. Your new life begins with his offer of forgiveness. When you went your way and ignored God, broke his commandments, and decided to place your will and desire at the center of your sheltered, personal universe, you offended God and stomped on his justice.

Somehow, despite all the evidence to the contrary, you assumed that you knew better than God did. Even though emptiness, loneliness, and emotional failure overwhelm your life, you are afraid to trust God, who knows you on a deeper, more personal level than anyone else.

Your New Life Is Not Dependent on Your Goodness

Salvation is a gift that God presents to those who have trusted him by faith. If you have surrendered your life to Christ, you now have the gift of eternal life, a life eternally spent in the presence of God. In Romans 4:7-8 (The Message Bible), Paul quotes David,

"Fortunate those whose crimes are carted off, whose sins are wiped clean from the slate. Fortunate the person against whom the Lord does not keep score."

Your salvation is not dependent on your personal goodness, a goodness that will never make the grade. If salvation were dependent on your good behavior, you would never attain it.

You can understand what Paul meant when he poetically cried out in Romans 7:24-25 (ESV),

"Wretched man that I am! Who will deliver me from this body of death? Thanks be to God through Jesus Christ our Lord!"

In his struggles to develop into the man he knew God wanted him to be, he came up short. He finally recognized that his efforts to become godly would always fail. He needed Christ to liberate him from his personal death-spiral.

In the same way as Paul, you need deliverance from the habits and character traits that separate you from God and prevent you from reaching your potential. Like him, you cannot do it without help. Fortunately, your relationship with God is not reliant on your acts of morality; it is dependent on the goodness of Christ.

You no longer have to live in fear of God rejecting you because of your failings and shortcomings. In essence, when God looks at you, He does not see your sin; he sees the righteousness of Jesus and "there is therefore now no condemnation for those who are in Christ Jesus." (Romans 8:1, ESV)

That means that when your conscience condemns you, causing you to feel lost, you can now know that God still loves you based on what Jesus has done. No matter how judged you feel, your feelings of judgment are a lie. God forgives you based on the righteous sacrifice of Jesus.

You Need God to Be the Focal Point of Your Life

Now you realize if something does not change, if you are unable to reverse your downward slide to destruction, there is no hope for you. You have made a mess of your life. Outwardly, it might not look like a disaster. Still, you know the truth.

Because you know the truth about you, you no longer want to be in charge of the breakdown of everything you hold dear. You are powerless to change, to live as though life has some higher purpose. The wrecked picture of a person that you have now become is the result of your failed attempts to chart your course, to do it your way.

You no longer want your way, the way of failure, addiction, and discouragement; you want God to be at the center of your life. You want to follow Christ. To follow Christ, you must give up your control of your life and surrender it to God. Ephesians 4:21-24 (The Message Bible) says,

"But that's no life for you. You learned Christ! My assumption is that you have paid careful attention to him, been well instructed in the truth precisely as we have it in Jesus. Since, then, we do not have the excuse of ignorance, everything—and I do mean everything—connected with that old way of life has to go. It's rotten through and through. Get rid of it!"

And then take on an entirely new way of life—a God-fashioned life, a life renewed from the inside and working itself into your conduct as God accurately reproduces his character in you."

To have a relationship with God, you must:

- Admit that you have excluded God from your life.
- Believe that Christ died and paid the price for your sins.
- Be willing to turn from your old life and embrace the new life of a Christ-follower.
- Surrender your life to Christ.

If you would like to surrender your life to Christ, you may begin by praying this prayer or one like it:

My Heavenly Father, I know I have made a mess of my life and rebelled against your authority over me. I now give up my old life and turn it over to you. Thank you that Jesus died for my sins so that I might have a relationship with you. Make me into a new person. In the name of Jesus, I pray. Amen.

When it comes to personal growth and change, God is the God of second chances, third chances, fourth chances, and so forth. He sees all of your shortcomings, character flaws, and attitudes of rebellion; but his overflowing love has drenched you with the goodness of Christ. You are accepted.

You need not be fearful that God will cast you away because you fail to measure up to his standards. Remember, God is love. Therefore, his love for you, not fear of judgment, is your incentive to change and grow and to fulfill his purpose for your life. Because of his love, you never have to surrender to the finality of failure and sin. His love picks you up, places you back on your feet, and compels you to live for Him.

"For Christ's love compels us . . . ."
(II Corinthians 5:17, NIV)

Conclusion

If you prayed this prayer and meant it with all your heart, you have taken the first step in your journey of becoming the man or woman God created you to be. You are on the verge of defeating your addiction and getting your life back.

Congratulations! You will not regret your decision. As you live your life, you will look back on this day with increasing fondness. Make sure you tell someone what God has done for you.

Sign up for a free workbook for
Winning the Addiction Battle
www.winningtheaddictionbattle.com

God's Purpose for Your Life

God has a purpose for your life. His purpose for you is not unique or unusual. It is not something that you have to discover through study, reading books, or signing into rehab.

It may feel like your addiction has caused God to abandon you, that he has given up on you and left you to finish your journey of self-destruction without any interference from him. It is hard to see the purpose for your life in the midst of madness and ruin.

God can use your past to accomplish his purpose for your life.

It is important for you to know that God is using both the good and bad experiences of your life as a tool to bring about his purpose for you. Your awareness that God is already working to accomplish his purpose for you can help you see beyond the daily grind of life and move from despair to hope. It strengthens you when you feel tempted to quit. It enables you to have a positive perspective on God's activities and work, to view your individual life as an unfinished canvas used by the master artist for painting a portrait of Christ.

Recently, after six years of hard work, one of my mission startups failed. It just did not fail; it self-destructed, nearly bankrupting me in the process. It will take more than a few years for me to pay off the debt I incurred trying to stabilize that mission.

Before it collapsed, I begged God to help me with the mission. The heavens seemed silent, cold, and unresponsive to my begging. I fasted; I tithed; I read the Scriptures. Things only became worse.

Some Christians chastised me for my lack of faith. If they had more faith than I did, I wondered, why was I the one risking everything to bring the Gospel to the poor? It hurt as they, from the sidelines, hurled at me their "outrageous arrows" of criticism and accusations. Fortunately, other Christians just loved me in my pain.

Despite knowing better, I felt like God had hung me out to dry. I was embarrassed, feeling like a failure and a loser.

Then it was over. The mission collapsed. It ended. It seemed as though all my efforts were in vain. We lost it all.

I went to work for a friend of mine who ran a similar ministry in another city. Despite his kindness to me, I felt humiliated, like an outcast, unfit for usefulness.

Soon, after much rigorous self-examination, I began to see more clearly the mistakes I had made. I finally understood that the mission's failure was my fault. God was completely innocent. This discovery taught me more about starting missions than all my successful mission plants combined. I was glad to know the truth. My prayer is that it will pave the way for the success of future plants in places of great need.

More importantly, the whole process taught me a significant truth about God. I learned that he is not a shallow friend who will quickly surrender his purpose for me by granting answers to prayers that hinder my spiritual growth and the development of Christlikeness in my life. He loved me too much to see me spoiled and puffed-up by easy success and achievement. God is not interested in shortcuts. For Him, the journey is just as important as the destination. The journey prepares us for ministry and abundant living.

The journey is also God's method for shaping your life into his purpose for you. From God's perspective, his purpose for your life is not a task for you to accomplish or some impressive scheme to change the world. It is not some great achievement or the founding of an enterprise to right some social evil. It is more subtle than that. In Romans 8:28-29 (The Message Bible), we read,

> "That is why we can be so sure that every detail in our lives of love for God is worked into something good. God knew what he was doing from the very beginning. He decided from the outset to shape the lives of those who love him along the same lines as the life of his Son."

All of us share this common purpose: to be more like Christ in our daily living, thinking, and attitudes. God's purpose for you is that you become more like Christ with each passing day.

Fulfilling God's purpose for your life by becoming more like Christ in your character, attitudes, and focus is essential for your goal of beating addiction. You cannot defeat addiction with a frontal assault. Even if you can win a victory, in most cases it will be fleeting and eventually reversed by a counter attack. Success will only come when you undermine the foundation of addiction.

When you change who you are as a person, you destroy addiction's foundational hold on your life. In Matthew 15:18-19 (The Message Bible), Jesus said,

"But what comes out of the mouth gets its start in the heart. It's from the heart that we vomit up evil arguments, murders, adulteries, fornications, thefts, lies, and cussing. That's what pollutes."

What Jesus is saying is that your actions flow from your inner being, your identity as a person. Christ-like behavior is the result of a Christ-like inner self. Changing your inner self is the key to chasing addiction from your life.

The process of fulfilling God's purpose for your life is also his method of preparing you for your future. As you become more like Christ, you are better equipped to face the rigors of life and survive its successes and failures. It will affect every area of your life, including your friends, family, acquaintances, and even strangers. Out of your purpose will flow God's calling for your life.

Becoming more Christ-like is not an instantaneous event. Just because you surrender to Christ does not mean your victory over addiction is instantaneous. In my twenty-seven years of working with men and women held prisoner by addiction, I have only seen this happen a few times. Do not count on it happening for you. Prepare yourself for the long haul. It took time for you to get into the trouble that now consumes your life; it will also take some time to untangle yourself from addiction's deceitful tentacles.

In this book, I lay out for you a plan that will help you destroy your addiction. The program prepares you to be receptive to the work the Holy Spirit wants to do in your life. The Holy Spirit is the real change-maker in your life. You do not have to do it alone. Fighting your addiction is a partnership between you and God.

God uses many methods to effect transformation in your life. He uses your successes, failures, experiences during your addiction, mistakes, bad behavior, church, Bible Study, prayer, friends, and enemies to make changes in your life. With God, nothing is wasted. He uses everything to accomplish his purpose for you.

That means that God uses the totality of your life to construct the image of Christ in you. He is a master artist. Even now as you read this, he is painting a portrait of Christ on the canvas of your heart. Your victory over your addiction is only a matter of time. He will not fail you.

Sign up for a free workbook for
Winning the Addiction Battle
www.winningtheaddictionbattle.com

Part Three: The Image of Christ

In the next three chapters, I will give you some examples of what the image of Christ looks like in real life. I want to give you enough information on this subject to help you understand more clearly what God's purpose for your life looks like in real time.

You cannot simply will, study, or force your life to reflect the image of Christ. Although it is important to understand the personality and character of Christ, you must never forget that the attainment of his image is a process and not a one-time event. Reading these chapters will clarify for you the exact nature and direction of the work God is doing in your life.

I do not want to bog you down with an exhaustive study of the character of Christ. You will spend the rest of your life trying to grasp the depth of his personality. I am going to focus on three of His character traits that, if developed in your life, will help you win your battle with addiction.

The three character traits are:

- Forgiveness
- Service
- Humility

As you read these chapters, ask God to use them in your life to change you and help you grow as a person.

Quit Drinking the Poison of Unforgiveness

In 2001, the board of directors of a multi-million dollar mission in the Midwest forced me to resign from my position as executive director. It was an awful experience. I felt utterly betrayed and defeated by the actions of several board members, men that I had trusted and considered as friends.

I remember waiting at my home for the board president to deliver personally my severance check. I could not wait to tell him what a jerk he was, to shout my indignation at such unjust treatment. How can a Christian be so unfair to a fellow believer? Anger and bitterness filled my heart; I wanted revenge. "How dare you treat me so disrespectfully? Don't you know how special I am?"

Then I remembered Jesus. In the ugliness of my pain and humiliation, I had left him on the side of the road, tossed him aside like a piece of trash. How could I forget the God who, set aside his glory, renounced his power and throne, surrounded himself with the dregs of humanity, labored to breathe under the tormentor's lash and was executed like a rabid dog?

Sometimes it is almost impossible to forgive someone who has wronged us. How can we forgive a person who has intentionally hurt us? It is even harder to forgive a blowhard who has murdered our reputation with false rumors or a spouse who has been unfaithful. Can we forgive a coworker who has used us as a stepping-stone to success, or a relative who has embarrassed the family with public displays of moral corruption? From the perspective of our shame and anger, these kinds of people just do not deserve our forgiveness.

Fortunately, Jesus understands our feelings and is sympathetic to our plight. He has been there! Imagine how he felt when they tried and convicted him in an illegal trial and then sentenced him to death. Imagine the pain when friends and followers abandoned him, the religious rejected him, and the masses ridiculed him. Imagine the shame and humiliation of being publicly stripped naked and then nailed to an old piece of wood. Surely, those who conspired to have him killed deserved the vilest form of punishment, yet that was not the response of Jesus.

On the cross Jesus cried out, "Father, forgive them, for they know not what they do." (Luke 23:34, ESV) In this prayer, God exposes his heart to us. God forgives his enemies! Those who crucified the Lord were unworthy of forgiveness, yet his love was stronger than hate.

In Romans 5:8 (ESV) the Apostle Paul wrote, "But God shows his love for us in that while we were still sinners, Christ died for us." You and I put Jesus on that cross. Moreover, it was for our forgiveness that Jesus pleaded as the life flowed from his body. Because he has forgiven those of us who trust him, we, too, must forgive our enemies.

In Luke 11:4 (ESV), Jesus gave us an example of how we should pray. He said, ". . . and forgive us our sins, for we ourselves forgive everyone who is indebted to us." Christians forgive! It does not matter what wrong or injustice someone committed against you. It does not matter how badly you have been hurt, wounded, or slandered. Since God forgave you, he expects you to forgive those who wronged you. What would you do if God's judgment concerning you imitated your judgment against those who wronged you? If he applied your standard, I suspect you would never find forgiveness.

A man once told me that someone had so wronged him that he just could not find the heart to forgive her. Perhaps you can identify with his sentiment. Try as you might, you just cannot forgive someone in your life who has wronged you, causing you hurt and grief. You feel trapped in a vicious cycle of bitterness and anger, possessed by the memory of an offense that wounded your pride and jeopardized your future.

Who does your unwillingness to forgive hurt? Do you believe that the person who broke trust with you will lose sleep because of his or her treachery? Will his guilt torment his conscience, ruin his ability to succeed, and wreck his relationships? Most likely, your enemy has forgotten all about the wrong he committed against you. If he does think about it, he justifies his unfair behavior as a necessary reaction to what he considers your wrongdoing. He does not believe he mistreated you. Moreover, if he does, he probably does not care.

Unforgiveness is like serving yourself a lethal dose of poison and expecting your enemy to die.

Even worse, when you do not forgive, you surrender extraordinary power to the person who wronged you. As long as the actions of that person replay in your mind, the person who hurt you is still in control. You give your oppressor the tools to hold you hostage to events long since passed. Your memories become the venue by which your adversary continues to victimize you. He wins the battle without placing himself in jeopardy or risking public exposure.

Remember, forgiveness is not an emotional response to someone who has wronged you. You may never "feel" forgiving. Real forgiveness is behavioral and not emotional. When you forgive someone, you treat that person as though he never wronged you. Only Christ can give you the strength to behave in that manner. As you begin to forgive, you start to heal.

At the last moment, just before my betrayer arrived at my house, I remembered Jesus. As he exited his car and approached my front steps, his slumped shoulders, and downcast eyes revealed to me his discomfort about meeting with me. "Fred, I am so glad to see you." At that very moment, I realized that he was not my enemy. He was just as much a victim as I was. The thick tension that had choked the air began to dissipate as the healing power of Christ penetrated the anger and bitterness that threatened my sanity and future.

A lack of forgiveness toward someone who has wronged you will stop any spiritual growth you are experiencing right in its tracks.

Remember what Jesus prayed on the cross:

"Father, forgive them; they don't know what they're doing."
Luke 23:34 (The Message Bible)

He prayed for mercy for Judas, who betrayed him, his disciples who deserted him, the religious establishment that convicted him in an illegal trial, the political authorities who sentenced him without cause, and the Roman soldiers who drove the nails into his hands and feet. Did their betrayal and offense stop him from forgiving? What is stopping you?

As this point in your spiritual growth, you probably could make a long list of people who have wronged you. Go ahead and make your list. Once you are finished writing your list, ask yourself this one question about each person on the list: Is it worth it?

Would you rather not forgive them and live with your bitterness and anger? On the other hand, would you rather forgive them and move on with your life?

Maybe it is time to rip up your list.

Changed by Your Service to Others

"He laid aside his outer garments, and taking a towel, tied it around his waist. Then he poured water into a basin and began to wash the disciples' feet and to wipe them with the towel that was wrapped around him."
John 13:4-5 (ESV)

"When he had washed their feet and put on his outer garments and resumed his place, he said to them, "Do you understand what I have done to you? You call me Teacher and Lord, and you are right, for so I am. If I then, your Lord and Teacher, have washed your feet, you also ought to wash one another's feet. For I have given you an example, that you also should do just as I have done to you. Truly, truly, I say to you, a servant is not greater than his master, nor is a messenger greater than the one who sent him. If you know these things, blessed are you if you do them."
(John 13:12-17, ESV)

It was my first soup kitchen in Bridgeport, Connecticut. I did most of the cooking while the volunteers from various churches served the food and did the after-dinner cleanup. While they were cleaning, I would spend time with the men, women, and children who came to the kitchen, each looking for a decent meal. The volunteers were fantastic. Not a single spot of dirt escaped their cleansing touch. They cleaned everything, except for the bathrooms.

It was the height of the AIDS epidemic. Stories of young people cut down in their prime by this deadly disease inundated the national and local news shows. It was also a time of ignorance and misinformation concerning the virus. Everyone was afraid of being infected. People shunned men and women with AIDS, afraid the same fate would befall them.

The volunteers were frightened of what might happen to them if they scrubbed the bathrooms. Liquid fecal matter covered the toilets, both inside and out, running down the sides. The odor was dreadful, almost unbearable. Mindful that many of the guests at our soup kitchen were IV drug users, the scene in the bathrooms conjured up their worst fears concerning the epidemic. For them, cleaning one of the toilets would mean putting their lives at risk, perhaps even threatening their families.

While I was a student, an older minister shared with me a story about his encounter with a toilet, a toilet that overflowed in the basement of the church he was pastoring. When it happened, this pastor was the only one in the building; everyone else had left for the day. The overflow required immediate action to prevent damage to the tile floor. He cleaned it up.

The minister concluded his story with this comment: "Imagine that, me, a man with a Ph.D., cleaning a toilet. While I was studying for my degree, who would have thought . . .?" He drifted off, driving home the point of his story. I am sure he was just trying to prepare me for the drudgery and mundane tasks often associated with the ministry.

His comments got me thinking. Maybe his ministry was the toilet, at least for that moment. Maybe because the heroic anecdotes of ministers and missionaries are so inspiring, we forget about the essence of who Jesus was as a person. Sometimes their stories, factual as they may be, cause us to believe that real ministry is about courageous acts of valor, excitement, adventure, huge crowds, crowded altars, and fame.

We love the preaching of Jesus, his words of wisdom and understanding that inspire us to live a higher life. We admire his courage as he faced down the professional religionists and the political forces that conspired against him. His healings and miracles, the manifestations of his power, the signs and wonders, all cause us to forsake the ordinary and focus on the spectacular.

Minus the cross, our dream is to be just like Jesus, high above the crowds and recognized as unique and gifted. We live in a day when fame is the ultimate measure of a person. Christians are not immune to this infection of the soul. We want to do something great for God so the common folk will recognize our special anointing, see us as numbered among the great ones and hang on every word of wisdom that flows from our mouths.

For many of us, life is all about people meeting our desires by serving and waiting on us. Relationships that do not satisfy our needs are cast aside as impediments to our happiness, as destructive forces that stifle our growth and prevent us from achieving our full potential. We judge new contacts through the prism of personal gain, benefits, and advancement. Our fame, resources, accomplishments, and influence define personal greatness.

Do not be fooled. This definition of greatness will corrupt your soul, extinguish any humility you may possess, and rip the fabric of connectedness that unites you with others. When you insist on others serving you and prioritizing your needs over those connected with you, you condemn yourself to living an inconsequential life, played out before an audience of one, yourself. You miss the real value of life—serving others. When the focus of your life is on having others meet your needs, your life can never become bigger than your limited skills and abilities.

For Jesus, serving was not just a specialized ministry; it was a lifestyle. The basin and towel from John 13 were not a sporadic activity stemming from a balanced lifestyle of public ministry and personal time. It was life itself! Jesus, the King of the universe, told his disciples in Matthew 20:28 that his focus in life was serving others. He did not enter our world for others to serve him and cater to his every need. If serving is central to the life of Jesus, maybe that explains the barrenness of fame, why prosperity in and of itself never satisfies.

Perhaps the toilet, shunned and neglected by the high and mighty, the fearful and timid, is the great place, the holy mountaintop, the altar of our God. Maybe you can only find the meaning of your life in the unexciting, dull tasks of service. It could be this is what Jesus meant when He told us that we could only find our lives by losing them.

When I lived in San Francisco, the Golden Gate Seminary invited me to speak to a group of first-year students about opportunities for service at my mission. These students were the best-of-the-best, talented, extremely bright, with promising futures ahead. They were eager to use their talents to advance the Kingdom of God.

Before I spoke, several leaders from other ministries presented to the group opportunities for them to serve at each of their ministries. Wow! The opportunities they offered were impressive, an acknowledgment of the unique giftedness possessed by each of these students. "If you volunteer at my ministry," they said, "You will have an opportunity to perfect the gifts God has given you. You can teach, preach, mentor, and counsel." The students ate it up. Who could blame them?

Then it was my turn to speak. "If you wish to serve at our mission, you must start by cleaning toilets. After you have proven yourself faithful at cleaning toilets, we'll look for other opportunities for you." Only one person volunteered to serve at our mission from that group.

I know you must think I am obsessed with toilets. Frankly, I hate cleaning toilets. I can think of far more productive things to do. In spite of that, I believe cleaning toilets is the modern version of washing feet. At first, it is a humbling experience, an apparent waste of my giftedness. But then again, maybe a humbling experience is what I need to enhance my gifts. Perhaps washing toilets are closer to the heart of Jesus than preaching a great sermon.

Sometimes we treat our neglect of menial service as just good leadership. After all, as leaders, delegating lesser tasks helps us focus on the things that are more in harmony with our abilities. Did not Paul teach us that we all have different gifts?

Remember what Jesus said after He washed the feet of the disciples:

"If I then, your Lord and Teacher, have washed your feet, you also ought to wash one another's feet. For I have given you an example, that you also should do just as I have done to you. Truly, truly, I say to you, a servant is not greater than his master, nor is a messenger greater than the one who sent him."
(John 13:14-16 ESV)

Are you more talented and gifted than Jesus? Was it a waste of his talent to wash their feet? When Jesus washed their feet, did that mean that he had delegation issues? Perhaps Jesus was not as competent a leader as you are. As I read Acts 6, I sometimes wonder if the apostles forgot the lesson of Jesus stripped of His outer clothing, wrapped in a towel, on His knees, washing the sand and caked-on dirt off their feet.

Most men and women only want to serve if they will receive an immediate personal blessing for their efforts. Without that blessing, they have little tolerance or staying power to continue volunteering at that ministry. Eventually, they move on to something more exciting and fulfilling. Of course, there are marvelous exceptions.

What if the most mundane and menial task is God's method of transforming your life? What if washing a toilet has the power to make you more like Jesus. Maybe it is a necessary step for becoming more powerful and compelling when you serve in a more noticeable ministry task.

Service Can Change Your Life

I know that many of your problems are severe, consuming vast amounts of time, thoughts, and conversations. Your problems can become an obsession, consume all your focus, and drive everyone around you crazy. Eventually, people tire of being around you, tire of listening to your daily recital of wrongs committed against you, and tire of hearing the same thing repeatedly. Left unchecked, you can become somewhat neurotic, unable to move on and grow as a person.

However, if you have problems in your life, and who does not, that does not mean you cannot try to find a solution that will fix the problem. You should do everything you can, including bringing the matter to God, to find a solution that will make things right. Unfortunately, not every problem is fixable. Some problems are irreversible, causing you much pain and hurt. As difficult as it may be, the solution is not dropping out of life and curling up in the fetal position. You must go on with your life.

Service to others helps you put your life in perspective. Even though your problems may be gigantic, helping others who suffer and need advice and support can get you out of your painful rut and deliver you from obsessing over yourself. When you are involved in something bigger than your life, your perception of life's meaning for you begins to grow and mature. You begin to trade your self-centeredness and focus on the wrongs committed against you for a life of service. In the loss of your personal obsessions, you will finally discover joy.

You will never change or beat addiction if the entire concentration of your life is on you. Even in your devotional life, the focus is on God and his purpose and vision for you. Purpose and vision always end in service. Service then comes full circle, because in reality, when you serve humanity, you are serving God.

In Matthew 25:34-40 (ESV), we read,

"Then the King will say to those on his right, 'Come, you who are blessed by my Father, inherit the kingdom prepared for you from the foundation of the world. For I was hungry and you gave me food, I was thirsty and you gave me drink, I was a stranger and you welcomed me, I was naked and you clothed me, I was sick and you visited me, I was in prison and you came to me.'

Then the righteous will answer him, saying, 'Lord, when did we see you hungry and feed you, or thirsty and give you drink? And when did we see you a stranger and welcome you, or naked and clothe you? And when did we see you sick or in prison and visit you?' And the King will answer them, 'Truly, I say to you, as you did it to one of the least of these my brothers, you did it to me'. "

You serve the King of Glory by helping the needy, the hurting, and the broken. He so intimately identifies with the brokenhearted that he proclaims that your service to them is the same as service to him. Whatever your giftedness may be, it must always include service to the poor, a theme echoed throughout the Old and New Testaments. According to the Bible, nations must give an account of themselves concerning their service to the poor.

In one sense, service is another way of connecting with God. That connection changes you. You may not be able to pray all day, but you can find multiple ways to connect your life with God. Service is another way you can hang out with God.

The more important you think you are, the more you need to wash toilets. Being in the limelight can become the means to your destruction. Maybe that is why one of the last things Jesus had taught his disciples before he went to the cross was the lesson of the basin and the towel. On the day of Pentecost, they became instant celebrities. The minute someone tells you what a great person you have become, be on guard. Do not listen to them. Listen to Jesus.

Start serving God today. In your service, you will find the meaning of your life. It will change you.

Humility and Recovery

"Think of yourselves the way Christ Jesus thought of himself. He had equal status with God but didn't think so much of himself that he had to cling to the advantages of that status no matter what. Not at all. When the time came, he set aside the privileges of deity and took on the status of a slave, became human! Having become human, he stayed human. It was an incredibly humbling process. He didn't claim special privileges. Instead, he lived a selfless, obedient life and then died a selfless, obedient death—and the worst kind of death at that—a crucifixion."
Philippians 2:5-8 (The Message Bible)

"A woman is sleeping in one of the back bedrooms. I tried to wake her up, but she won't budge." These words greeted me one morning upon my arrival at our new building that now belonged to the Bridgeport Rescue Mission in Connecticut. We had only been in the building for a couple of days. The previous night was my first night away from the building after spending a rough couple of days securing the premises after taking possession of it from a street gang.

"Who is she?" I asked. No one knew her name or the reason for her presence at the mission. She was in a back room that was isolated from the rest of the rooms.

Taking one of the men with me, I made a beeline for the bedroom that was now home to a stranger. When I opened the door into her room, the first thing I noticed was the broken window and the glass scattered on the bed all around our uninvited guest. She was sound asleep.

"What is your name?" I asked. I used my authoritative voice. Waking from a sound sleep, she replied, "Maria." As she sat up, she rubbed her eyes and then looked directly at me. She looked confused and seemed to be a little nervous.

"Who are you?" she asked. I told her my name. I also told her that the building was now home to a Christian mission that focused on helping men get off the streets and beat their addictions. I asked her to leave while informing her that it was impossible for a woman to stay in a building that was housing a Christian program for men. We fed her breakfast and sent her on her way.

Later that day, I fed a large group of people in a place called Washington Park. The park was notorious for drug dealing, crime, and prostitution. My volunteers did the actual serving while I interacted with the men, women, and children who were waiting in line for a meal.

After about thirty minutes of serving food, Maria got in the food line to get a plate of food. Afterward, she walked over to me and began to tell me her story. Maria was a prostitute.

Without going into all the sordid details, I can tell you that Maria's story was both depressing and scary. First, I learned that her real name was Luz. Maria was her daughter's name. Earlier that day I had startled her when I asked for her name. Thinking I was a cop, out of self-protection, she lied.

Luz was addicted to both crack/cocaine and heroin. To feed her addiction, she became a prostitute. As you know, addiction can be a deadly and dangerous habit.

She was unaware that the gang that once held possession of our building was no longer in control. She would sometimes sleep in one of the rooms when she ran out of other options for a place to stay. When she found the door locked, she broke one of the windows to gain entry.

She also told me with pride about her four beautiful children: Maria, Anais, Luis, and Angelina. Because of her addictive lifestyle, she had placed the children with relatives and friends at various locations in the city. I did not know it at the time, but later I learned that the children were living in hazardous and unhealthy settings.

Several days later in front of our building, I saw Luz get into a fistfight with another prostitute named Janice. Luz's superior size enabled her to get the best of Janice.

Luz would often visit my office so that we could talk. She was always very respectful and never out of line with me. She just needed a sympathetic ear to listen to all her troubles.

One day, Luz came to me for help. She wanted to kick heroin, but there was no place for her to go. She needed someone to help her do it cold turkey. I cordoned off a section of the building for her. I brought my wife in to help.

It was not a pretty site, but she completed her detox. After a few days, she started to get her strength back. She began to look like a new woman.

By that time, our ministry started to blow up with people coming to us for help. Men and women were lining up to talk to me about Jesus. In my life, I had never seen anything like it before. Gang members, addicts, and prostitutes were surrendering to Jesus in large numbers.

It got so crazy that I could not talk to everyone personally. I told Tammy to take Luz to one of the back rooms and lead her to Jesus. "How do you know she's ready?" she nervously asked. "She's ready," I exclaimed. "They're all ready. God is at work!"

Tammy took Luz to one of the rooms in the back. Luz was ready. God was already at work in her life. As Tammy began to explain the Gospel to her, Luz broke down and gave her life to Christ. It was incredible.

The change in Luz was nothing short of miraculous. She started bringing other women to our mission to hear the same story that had changed her life, the story of the Jesus, who even loves prostitutes. They had come to believe they were beyond love. Who could love a prostitute? Jesus could!

Several weeks later, two women showed up at our front door and asked for help. Like Luz, they were prostitutes with an addiction to heroin. We agreed to help them.

Luz insisted on taking care of them. Without any prodding from us, she cleaned up their vomit, washed their clothes, and wiped the sweat off their faces. She served them.

Luz's acts of service were the personification of the word humility. She had spent much of her life focused on herself. Her desire for drugs, men, and personal happiness had consumed her life. When she was on the streets, she was full of herself, filled with pride, completely oblivious to anyone else but herself.

When Christ came into her life, it changed everything. It was no longer about Luz; it was about meeting someone else's need. Something had changed. Now it was about cleaning up the vomit of two AIDS-infected hookers who had spent years living under a bridge.

If asked, I am sure Luz could not have provided a proper definition of the word humility. I am not even sure she was aware of the changes that were taking place in her life because of her newfound relationship with Christ. Her act of service to the two women detoxing was not some bold attempt by her to grab humility by the tale and subdue it, to make it her own. She was not acting humble; she was humble.

Her new relationship with Christ started her on a journey that was beginning to change her whole perception of life. Her actions were her first response to the internal changes that were taking place within her through the work of the Holy Spirit. God was in the process of changing Luz to reflect the image of Christ in her life.

The Humility of Christ

The verses you read at the beginning of this chapter focus on the humility of Christ. The starting point for defining humility is Christ. If you start anywhere else, your definition will end up corrupted by false understandings that reflect our contemporary culture instead of the personality of Christ.

Without digging too deeply into the nature of Christ, we begin by looking at the price Jesus paid to be born. Our verses state,

"He had equal status with God . . . ."

The birth of Jesus was not the beginning of his life. We read in these verses that Jesus was God. Imagine for a moment what things were like for him before he was born. He was:

- The King of kings
- Surrounded and worshiped by adoring angels
- All-powerful
- All knowing
- The Creator of the universe and everything in it
- Eternally alive, with no beginning or end
- All loving
- Perfect in all things
- In a place without tears, pain, sorrow, or death

These verses say he gave it all up, everything, to be born as a human being.

"He had equal status with God but didn't think so much of himself that he had to cling to the advantages of that status no matter what. Not at all. When the time came, he set aside the privileges of deity and took on the status of a slave, became human! Having become human, he stayed human. It was an incredibly humbling process. He didn't claim special privileges."

His birth as a human being changed everything. It was the surrender of his position, power, and safety. He went from:

- Total security to dependence for survival on an adolescent peasant girl in some remote outpost of the Roman Empire
- Total comfort to a roughly fashioned animal feeding trough (manger) as a crib

- Being clothed in majesty to being dressed in strips of cloth
- Total power to the weakness of being born as a baby

In his life on earth, his association with the outcast and rejected was a picture of his humility in action. His friends included prostitutes, tax collectors, drunkards, and other men and women outside the norm of society. At his death, two convicted thieves were by his side.

He willingly lowered Himself to become weak, dependent, and vilified; yet he was not a victim, carried along by circumstances beyond his control. Although he was in total control of his destiny, he freely chose the way of hardship and suffering, without regard for his reputation or safety.

His humility expressed itself in obedience. The result of his submission was the agony of the cross, the ultimate humility for the Creator of the universe. The night before they crucified him, while in the Garden of Gethsemane, he prayed,

"Going a little ahead, he fell on his face, praying, 'My Father, if there is any way, get me out of this. But please, not what I want. You, what do you want'?"
Matthew 26:39 (The Message Bible)

"He then left them a second time. Again he prayed, 'My Father, if there is no other way than this, drinking this cup to the dregs, I'm ready. Do it your way'."
Matthew 26:42 (The Message Bible)

Within him was the power to save his life and avoid the public humiliation of the cross.

"Instead, he lived a selfless, obedient life and then died a selfless, obedient death—and the worst kind of death at that—a crucifixion."
Philippians 2:8 (The Message Bible)

When he made his choices, he placed your welfare above his own. His decision to go to the cross is your means of deliverance from the scourge of addiction. His death means a new life and brand new world for you. His choice will help you get your life back.

The Image of Humility in Your Life

In this section, I am going to delve deeper into humility by exploring the following questions:

1) What is humility?
2) Is it something you can attain by effort?
3) How does humility help you defeat addiction?

What is humility?

In our culture, many people view humility as personal weakness personified. According to the opinion of most, humble men and women are punching bags for the powerful. They lack the courage to stand up for themselves and assert their will in the face of adversity or conflict. They are pathetic, without self-confidence, unable to enforce their will because of a low self-esteem.

When I was in college, Dr. Bill Blevins, my New Testament professor, gave me a definition of humility that stuck with me all these years. He said,

"Humility is your confession, which despite all the positive talents and abilities you may possess, that you still need God to make your life whole."

C.S. Lewis, a famous Christian author, said in his book Mere Christianity:

[3]*"Humility is not thinking less of yourself; it is thinking of yourself less."*

In previous chapters, I spoke with you about the necessity of discovering and admitting the truth about you. In one sense, the opposite of humility is a cover-up. Your pride can prevent you from ever facing the truth about you. You lie to yourself, effectively

---

[3] Lewis, C. S. "Humility Is Not Thinking Less of Yourself; It Is Thinking of Yourself Less." *Mere Christianity*. New York: MacMillan Pub., 1952. N. pag. Print.

covering up the truth and stopping your personal growth right in its tracks.

The first stage of humility is your admission that you need help to defeat your addiction. Your confession of helplessness in your battle to change your life is a critical step in your desire to become a new person. Your admission of need is an act of true humility.

Refusing to humble yourself by not acknowledging your need for help prolongs your insane lifestyle and increases the chance of doing permanent damage to your life. Pride prevents you from getting your life back; it robs you of your future and sentences you to an endless cycle of relapse and recovery.

"First pride, then the crash—the bigger the ego, the harder the fall."
Proverbs 16:18 (The Message Bible)

Embracing humility unleashes God's power in your life. When you admit you need God to make you whole, you are setting the stage for God's entrance into your life.

"Humble yourselves before the Lord, and he will lift you up."
James 4:10 (NIV)

Whereas pride keeps you trapped in your addiction, humility opens the door for recovery and a new life. Without humility, there is no hope for you.

Is humility something that you can attain by effort?

The Bible instructs us to pursue humility. In I Peter 5:5-7 (ESV) we read,

". . . Clothe yourselves, all of you, with humility toward one another, for "God opposes the proud but gives grace to the humble." Humble yourselves, therefore, under the mighty hand of God so that at the proper time he may exalt you, casting all your anxieties on him, because he cares for you."

Humility has three essential parts:

- Your attitude about you

- Your relationship with God
- Your relationship with other people

As these three points relate to humility, you can make intentional decisions that will produce humility in your life. I have often heard people say that if you are aware of your humility, then you are no longer humble, but proud. Perhaps there is some truth to that. Notwithstanding, the Bible instructs us throughout the Old and New Testament to humble ourselves. It also promises that God will reward your humility.

Your Attitude About You

In Romans 12:3 (ESV), we read,

"For by the grace given me I say to everyone of you: Do not think of yourself more highly than you ought, but rather think of yourself with sober judgment, in accordance with the faith God has distributed to each of you."

In the addiction battle, self-confidence is dangerous. Take a realistic assessment of your past efforts to defeat your addiction. Even if you were able to stay clean for a period, it did not last. Eventually, you relapsed and ended up returning to your captivity and self-imposed prison.

Several years ago, I had a conversation with a young woman about entering our residential recovery program. Crack/cocaine had taken possession of her life. She spent her nights sleeping on a friend's couch and eating her meals at my soup kitchen. Life was not working out for her.

My efforts to help her were unsuccessful. She told me she did not need help with her addiction. Several years before our conversation, she had quit using crack without the aid of anyone else. She did it on her own. If she could quit once without help, she could do it again. She thought she could stop anytime she got ready to quit.

I tried to explain to her that her self-help method had not worked. After all, if it had worked, why was she back on drugs again? It was evident that she could not remain drug-free without help. Despite all the evidence to the contrary, she could not bring herself to admit her need for help. More than likely, she was not ready to change her life. Apparently, she had not suffered enough.

When your confidence is completely in you, you miss valuable resources and help necessary for you to succeed. It is important to understand your limitations. Do not fall victim to the old Napoleon Hill quote: "What the mind of man can conceive and believe, he will achieve." At its most basic level, it is untrue. It is nothing more than positive-thinking mumbo-jumbo.

For instance, no matter how much I believe that I can play basketball in the NBA, it will never happen. Thinking positive thoughts will never overcome the limitations of my height. Some barriers are impossible to surmount.

Most of the time, Mr. Hill is quoted out of context. Throughout his books, he spells out, repeatedly, the necessity of aligning yourself with like-minded men and women who can help you achieve your goals. Success is hardly ever a solitary endeavor.

To have the right attitude about you means admitting by your words and actions that you lack sufficient strength and resources to battle your addiction. You need help. To be humble means, you are not too proud to ask for aid when you need it. Equally, your pride does not stand in the way of receiving help from someone who offers to provide you with assistance. Both of these are conscious decisions that only you can make.

As long as you continue to believe that you can win the addiction battle without help, you will never win. You will continue to shatter your life. Pursue humility by asking for help.

Your Relationship With God

"I am the vine; you are the branches. Whoever abides in me and I in him, he it is that bears much fruit, for apart from me you can do nothing."
John 15:5 (ESV)

In your pursuit of humility, your connection to God is an indispensable component of your battle to change your life. In this verse, Jesus explains that apart from him, real and lasting change is impossible. Life-change flows from our connection to him.

As you spent time with God, you become more like him in your thinking, actions, and motivations. He changes you from an addict to a person who reflects the image of Christ. He makes you into a godly man or woman, someone who lives life on a higher level than before. Addiction becomes a terrible memory, a former habit that no longer has the power to bind you to a life filled with self-destruction, disaster, and loneliness.

In this context, humility is recognizing that you need God to make you whole. Without God, you will never achieve the purpose for which he created you. Left to yourself, you live a counterfeit life, a life of cheap imitations and emptiness. Humility is reaching out to God for help to rebuild your life. Pursue humility by reaching out and connecting with God.

Your Relationship With Other People

'It shall not be so among you. But whoever would be great among you must be your servant, and whoever would be first among you must be your slave, even as the Son of Man came not to be served but to serve, and to give his life as a ransom for many."
Matthew 20:26-28 (ESV)

Greatness, according to Jesus, is serving others. Relationships should be all about the value you add to the lives of the men and women who are a part of your life. You look for ways to help them succeed and experience God's best for them.

As stated in a previous chapter, service is one of God's methods for helping you change your life. When you fail to serve others, you fail in your efforts to change you and become all that God intends for you to be. Pursue humility by serving others.

Humility is the springboard to a new life. It is an open invitation to God and others to help you change your life. Without it, you are stuck, reduced to self-effort and personal strength. No matter how great and important you think you might be, without humility you are deluded.

Conclusion

Humility is a process that grows with time. You do not have to be perfectly humble to get help from others or God. If you just open your heart to God, he will run to meet you. He will not abandon you to your addiction and mess.

If you want to have a deeper understanding of humility, study Jesus. His life is a perfect picture of humility.

As you live your life, the deeper your connection with God, the more humble you will become. Your humility will cause God to lift you to a higher place, leaving your addiction in the dust, a plague that bothers you no more.

Part Four: Surrender and Change

Real and lasting change in your life is dependent upon your submission to God. He only works in areas of your life that you have surrendered to him. Without surrender, you strip the power from your life. You will never experience God's personal best for you. You will end up living a life of unfulfilled dreams and expectations.

Most people find surrender to be a difficult bridge to cross. They are afraid of missing some great experience or desire. They do not trust God enough to believe he has their best interests at heart.

However, things should be different for you. You already know what it means to miss life's best. The wreckage of your life follows you wherever you go. Thus far, you have been unable to escape it. For you, surrender to God is your only hope. Your life experiences should be enough evidence to convince you that surrender is the only way out of your predicament.

I know from personal experience what it means to live a life not surrendered to God. I was always afraid that God's plan for me would never measure up to the plans I had for my future. My new life has proved me wrong. As I go forward in life, I have learned that God's plan for me is greater and more meaningful than anything I had ever conceived on my own.

I invite you to join me in my journey of surrender. Your life will never be the same.

Worship and Surrender

In a book about defeating addiction, you might wonder why I have written a chapter about worship. It is because worship of God and surrender are inseparable. In one sense, they are indistinguishable from each other. Worship and surrender are part of your battle plan for defeating addiction.

When you start looking for a church to attend, you will notice the music played and sung at each church is not always the same. Some may sing traditional hymns, others contemporary or Southern Gospel music.

The Bible is not specific about what kind of music to use while we worship. As we study the Bible, one thing is abundantly clear: music is a physical expression of our devotion to God. Throughout Scripture, singing, shouting, and playing musical instruments are an integral part of worship. Music focuses our attention on God and clears our mind of distractions. It should unite us as a body of believers.

However, worship is not limited to physical expressions of awe and religious passion. Surrendering our lives is the truest expression of our devotion to God. Paul, in his writings to the Christians in Rome, wrote,

> "So here's what I want you to do, God helping you: Take your everyday, ordinary life—your sleeping, eating, going-to-work, and walking-around life—and place it before God as an offering. Embracing what God does for you is the best thing you can do for him. Don't become so well-adjusted to your culture that you fit into it without even thinking. Instead, fix your attention on God. You'll be changed from the inside out. Readily recognize what he wants from you, and quickly respond to it. Unlike the culture around you, always dragging you down to its level of immaturity, God brings the best out of you, develops well-formed maturity in you."
> Romans 12:1-2 (The Message Bible)

In the verses above, the Apostle Paul pleads with us to present our lives as an offering to God. In the gospel of John, Chapter 4:23 (ESV), we read,

"But the hour is coming, and is now here, when the true worshipers will worship the Father in spirit and truth, for the Father is seeking such people to worship him."

Your surrender to God is a reflection of the reality of God's mercy in your life and his commitment to you and me. He abandoned his throne, position, power, honor, and glory to rescue you from your misery, despair, and separation from him. Then, in his ultimate act of surrender and dedication, he presented himself to the pagan Roman authorities and the hypocritical religious leaders as a sacrifice for your sins. His earthly life was a picture of pure mercy that ended in the destruction of his life on the cross.

Your primary motivation for surrender, i.e. worship, should be the bleeding Christ on the cross, the One wounded for your wrongdoings and numbered with the criminals. The cross was an act of total surrender. He held nothing back. The cross is the definition and meaning of the word surrender. It defines surrender as the overthrow of your self-directed will and its replacement with God's will.

Paul was writing this letter to Christians, yet he felt the need to remind them, to the point of even begging them, to surrender their lives to God. I find comfort knowing that the struggle of staying surrendered is not just a problem unique to me. The earliest Christians are my companions in this battle—your companions too.

Worship is not just a solitary, once-in-a-lifetime event. Worship is like the air you breathe. Without a constant supply of air, you suffocate and quickly die. For the Christian, life is worship, a daily surrender to God. Surrender is life, the key to growth and transformation.

Self-worship is an obstruction that blocks the power of God in your life. It prevents you from reaching your full potential, from experiencing the joy of God-focused worship and surrender. It demeans your dreams and hopes, causes you to settle for a life of disappointment, and forces you to value things and experiences that are more hurtful than helpful when viewed from the perspective of your whole lifetime. It leads to a life of regret and troubled memories of what might have been. It is a failure to be fully human.

The act of surrender, of true worship, always precedes change. It is a leading indicator of Christlikeness, of personal destiny accomplished by the power of God. Surrender is the entrance for God's rule to enter your life and destroy habits, addictions, and defects that plague your relationships and spoil your future.

Without surrender to God, your change is temporary. It rarely lasts. Before long, you will revert to your nightmares and addictions. Without surrender, your only hope for bringing change into your life is willpower, grim determination, and therapy that will never end. You spend your time in a ceaseless search for the root causes that ordained the flaws in your character. Without surrender, you are stuck; you are what you are.

James Surrendered Everything to Obtain the Object of His Desire

One night, as I sat behind my desk in my office at the mission, a young, uninvited man burst into my office and, with a mixture of pain and conviction, said, "Help me! I don't want to be this way anymore." With just a glance, you could tell that he was deeply troubled. He had the stench and appearance of a homeless man, the bloodshot eyes of a drunk, and the demeanor of a man desperate for help.

His name was James. Several days before, his wife, tired of his lies, his constant stealing of their rent money for buying drugs, and his neglect of her and the children, told him to get out of the house and not come back until he regained his sanity. For a drink of beer and a tiny rock called crack, James was willing to give up his job, his wife, his children, his home, his bathtub, his dignity, and his self-respect. He was ready to destroy his whole life to obtain the object of his desire.

That night in my office, James surrendered his life to Christ. Before that night, he had submitted his life to a substance that eventually destroyed everything of beauty and value in his life. When James surrendered to Christ, God gave him his life back, including his marriage. He eventually found a job and began to provide for his family. As further evidence of the power of surrender to God, God lifted James up from the gutter to leadership in his church.

Brokenness

The whole concept of brokenness is repulsive to most people. For many of us, the word brokenness is synonymous with personal destruction, ruin, loss, or failure. To be broken means that we have reached the limits of our individual talents and abilities; we have failed to obtain our goals; we cannot cut the mustard; we are inadequate; we have reached the end of ourselves.

In one sense, brokenness is the result of self-sufficiency and self-confidence. We conclude that we do not have the "right stuff" to accomplish our dreams and goals. Brokenness is at the end of effort. It is a realization that we need help beyond ourselves. It is recognition of personal or public failure. Brokenness can bring anguish and fear, feelings of instability and uncertainty, of personal dread concerning our future and even sometimes our reputation.

Brokenness is the sense of inadequacy and helplessness we experience after the death of someone we love, the breakup of our marriage, the loss of a job, the destruction of our finances, a moral failure or a business fiasco. Tragedies and failures contribute to our sense of failure and hopelessness, filling us with despair.

The positive lesson of brokenness is our understanding that despite all of our skills, intelligence, personal strengths, and public disguises, without God, we are nothing.

Brokenness is the starting point for God to change your life. Without it, your life can never grow beyond your personal strength and effort. With it, you are in a beautiful place, a place of new beginnings where God can begin his work of transformation in your life.

Your surrender to God is the result of your recognition that you cannot defeat addiction and your other character issues without his help. Submission means that you accept the superiority of God and his claim of authority over your life. In the defeat of your self-will, God requires nothing less than unconditional surrender.

What is brokenness? Does brokenness only occur after the complete loss of everything that you find meaningful? In one sense, brokenness is going deeper in your dependency on God. It means that your desire to go to another level with God is beyond your ability to accomplish, that there is some blockage beyond your power to remove.

Here are some examples of obstructions:

- Your marriage may not be in trouble yet, but it is stuck, more routine and comfort than exciting and surprising. Routine and comfort have caused you to take your spouse for granted. What you need is a marriage makeover, a new beginning. However, your rut is so deep you cannot escape.
- You are single. You have tried singles' groups, church groups, and even online dating sites. You are still lonely and alone. Some of you are miserable. You feel powerless to do anything about it. You have postponed happiness for some future date when you meet the right person.
- Your finances seem unfixable, more debt than income. Your feelings of stress and hopelessness are growing. All your plans to fix the situation fail.
- You are discouraged with God. The promises of Scripture seem to be for other people and not you. Where is God when you need Him?
- Some of you even feel as though God has abandoned you. It appears he does not care about your hurts,

disappointments, sadness, confusion, and discouragement. You still play the Christian game, but you are just pretending. You wear your Christian face to keep up appearances. You do not want others to know what you are thinking.
- Your children, maybe not all of them, have gone down a dangerous path. Their indiscretions have caused you to behave badly. You do not know how to regain the upper hand or at least control yourself.
- You are bored with life. It has become tedious, something to be endured and not enjoyed.
- Frustration with the future of our country has reached a boiling point. Nothing you do—vote, knock on doors, make donations, or pray—seems to make much of a lasting difference. It feels like it is over.

Are you satisfied with your level of surrender to God? I suspect, just like in my life, that your surrender has limits. In your quest for moderation and balance, you are afraid to cross certain lines. Why are you scared?

Are you afraid that if you completely surrender, God will carry out some horrid plan for your life? Do you trust Him enough to surrender completely, without conditions? If there are conditions, it is only a negotiated settlement, not surrender.

More Thoughts on Surrender

"For to me, to live is Christ and to die is gain."
Philippians 1:21 (ESV)

I want you to go deeper in your surrender to Christ. You were willing to lose everything for the sake of your addiction. Now take that same energy and self-sacrifice, and use it for God.

Recently I heard someone give a public testimony of how he had destroyed his life for a sip of gin. Even though I have heard many such stories, this one made me think about my life. This person was willing to lose everything for a sip of gin, to preside over the wholesale destruction of everything important to him so he could get high.

Often the other side of someone's personal story encourages us with tales of restored reputations and honor, decent jobs and new homes, the mending of broken relationships, and successful ministry within the church. A great testimony is one that documents the transformation of insanity to sanity, outcast to respectability, and the restoration of normality.

As I listened to this person's testimony, I was surprised at what he was willing to lose so that he could get high. His statement prompted me to wonder: Does our understanding of salvation rob us of our passion and our willingness to suffer loss for the sake of the Gospel? Has the Gospel become merely a ticket to the American dream? What are we willing to give up for the Gospel?

The Apostle Paul lost his reputation, his position in the community, his family, his freedom, and eventually his life. For the sake of the Gospel, as he proclaimed in Philippians Chapter 3, he lost everything. Paul's testimony was the story of someone who had it all and then, because of his commitment to Christ, suffered the loss of everything he had worked so hard to achieve.

Paul spent his early adult years as a member of the professional religionist class. He was a highly respected member of his community. He had position, prestige, security, and power.

When Christianity first came on the scene, Paul felt frightened by its potential impact on his Jewish faith. In response, he participated in a severe persecution of the early church. He was an enthusiastic advocate of the stoning of Stephen, one of the early church leaders. His activities against the church were both fearsome and effective.

His success in battling the Christian heresy prompted the Jewish leadership to send him to a city called Damascus. His job was to bring back any Jew who had converted to Christianity. On the way to Damascus, he met Jesus. That encounter with Jesus transformed his whole way of looking at life. Before that meeting, he was certain that Jesus had died at his crucifixion. Now he knew he was alive. After that day, Paul was never the same again.

Jesus gave him a new assignment. He was to become a preacher, a church planter, a missionary, and a witness to the world on behalf of Jesus. Because of this huge change in his life, Paul eventually lost everything—his position, power, recognition in the community, resources, health, and ultimately his life. Paul described his new role as being like "the scum of the earth."

If respectability is the principal fruit of the Gospel, then it is easy to see why Christianity is declining in power and influence. We are no longer world-changers, but instead, maintainers of the status quo. Somehow, we have come to believe that successful proclamation of the Gospel includes demonstrating to the world that Jesus will make all our pre-conversion hopes and dreams come true.

Instead, we should emphasize the necessity of a transformation in a person's worldview as they grow in their relationship with Christ. The real proclamation of the Gospel impassions a person to surrender their hopes and dreams, their possessions and money, their future and security, and even their health and life.

There is a belief in the Christian community that teaches resources always precede vision. I remember many years ago when I started planting missions, being told, "Young man, you need to be prudent, wise, and accountable to God and man." I understood the concept of accountability, but it soon became evident that the words prudent and wise were coded words for squelching the vision God had given me for my life and ministry. Their caution and fear shaped their actions, causing them to conclude that unless God provides the means in advance, it was too risky to invest money, reputation, and time in a ministry that might fail.

When my dad was alive, he often said to me, "Son, when are you going to get a real job?" He knew that in my startups, we often went months without a paycheck. He continued, "Most ministers, when they sense that God is calling them to a new ministry, move to more prominent churches with bigger parsonages and larger salaries. But you, Son, it's always a pit." I said slowly, "I know, Dad. I guess I'm downwardly mobile."

I must admit, I have experienced more than my fair share of failure in ministry. My failures and successes have wrecked my finances repeatedly, at times plunging me deeply into debt. My clothing is often old and worn; my car is always in need of repair. My reputation goes up and down, depending on how well or not so well our latest startup is doing. I sure hope social security is still functioning when I get too old to work.

I still remember what my life was like when I was not following Christ. For me, no price was too steep to pay for what I considered the sheer joy of drinking and partying. For a season, I enjoyed it so much that I was willing to endure the consequences of my foolishness. It eventually destroyed me. Now, the big question in my life is this: Am I willing to surrender everything I have, my reputation, my money, my future and even my life, so that my life will bring glory to God?

Furthermore, does this mean I only need to surrender harmful habits and behaviors? In my submission to Christ, I relinquished my drunkenness, lying, recklessness, and other destructive practices that proved to be so damaging to my life. So now, according to most, I am sane, with an exciting testimony of transformation to prove it.

If an addict is willing to oversee the wholesale destruction of his or her life for a fix or a drink, why is it that many Christians are lukewarm, unduly cautious and afraid to make adjustments in their lives that endanger the orderliness of their lifestyle? Why have we jettisoned the biblical injunctions of "losing our lives to find them," "taking up our crosses," and "surrendering our advantages and strengths to know Christ"?

Perhaps the blessings in our lives have become barriers to experiencing the richness of the benefits that are the consequence of a surrendered life. I believe that we have settled for phony blessings that ultimately will leave us empty and barren. In our attempts to achieve security and balance, we have missed the real foundation of a fulfilling life. We have forgotten that Jesus is the unshakable rock. Maybe that explains why so many Christians live unsatisfied lives.

Perhaps this is true for you. The promises in Scripture have failed to materialize in your life, causing you to doubt the dependability of God's love and provision for you. No matter how much you try, you cannot seem to connect with God. Your faith has deteriorated into a Sunday ritual, completely inadequate for the real stuff of life.

So instead of soaring with the eagles, you have settled for a normal existence—financial stability, a mortgage, a family, and a decent job. All of these things do have substantial value, but in reality, they will never bring you the joy that is the fruit of a surrendered life. Life is more than stability and balance. In fact, balance is overrated. Life is Christ. In Philippians 1:21 (ESV), the Apostle Paul wrote, "For to me, to live is Christ and to die is gain."

For so many of us, surrender is a frightful thing. We are afraid that we might miss the good things life offers if we just leave it up to God. In reality, God is not a part of the process that we use to determine our plans for the future. We only invite him to bless our plans and make them a reality after we have outlined our goals and dreams.

This approach reveals our deep-seated belief that we know what is best for our lives. Without saying it, we assume that complete surrender to God would be too high a price to pay. In other words, we do not trust God to have a plan for our lives that will satisfy our deepest longings and needs. Our lack of faith makes us afraid to pay any price for our relationship with God.

Surrender Has a Price

Several years ago, I brought a message to the men in my addiction program on the subject of "Paying the Price for Your Dream." My Scripture verse was Romans 15:20 (ESV). It says, ". . . and thus I make it my ambition to preach the gospel, not where Christ has already been named, lest I build on someone else's foundation. . . ."

Paul's dream was to preach the Gospel to men and women who had not heard the Gospel. To achieve that dream or calling, he was willing to endure hardships, beatings, stoning and incarceration, rumors concerning his character, hunger, sleeplessness, depression, stress, and danger. In the end, they beheaded him, hoping to end his influence and curtail the expansion of Christianity.

From my earliest years as a Christian, I dreamed of doing something great for God, something that would have a significant impact on the advancement of God's kingdom. I pictured huge crowds, thousands of filled-out salvation cards, and national recognition. Mature reflection has forced me to conclude that my vision may have been more about being great, rather than doing something great that brought honor to God.

As I watched others achieve their dreams of success in ministry, I began to see myself as a Lazarus, exiled from the banquet table, scorned as one covered by festered sores, desperate for scraps of respect from those feasting at the table of fame and achievement. I tried not to be jealous; but I felt as though God had abandoned me to a lesser endeavor, life among the outcasts, the poor, and the despised.

As I previously stated, my wife and I have spearheaded the planting of missions in various cities across the United States. Both of us have paid a considerable price for this to happen. We have sacrificed hundreds of thousands of dollars of our money, often leaving little for our personal expenses. We have known poverty and danger. In front of my house, in an attempt to kill me, several gang members fired five shots at me. Addicts and criminals have made dozens of death threats against me. A street gang in Bridgeport, Connecticut, put out a death contract on me. Often I wondered if I would even see the next day. I have lived with constant stress and concern about the mission's finances, my finances, the safety of my family, and the success of the men and women in my programs. Sometimes I battle bouts of depression, struggling to keep going when the odds seem so stacked against us.

As I was preaching to the men about the sacrifices that Paul made to accomplish his dream, it suddenly hit me: I am doing something great for God. I am not great, not by any stretch of the imagination. Perhaps I lack the talent of many higher souls, men and women drenched with the anointing of God's blessing, presence, and power. Since I lack the ability of others, I know I have no choice but to rely on God for rescue from my self-inflicted troubles.

Jesus tells the story of a man who went on a journey and entrusted his property to his servants. To one servant he gave five talents of money (a talent was worth more than a thousand dollars), to another two talents, and to another one, according to each one's ability. When he returned, he judged their faithfulness by how well they used the resources he provided them before beginning his journey.

I have spent much of my life getting into trouble for God. Someone with greater talent and ability would have seen the foolishness of my behavior and chosen a much wiser path. Sadly, I have concluded that I am only a one-talent man.

For whatever reason, when we arrive at a new city, I rarely have enough money to start a mission. Usually within a short period, I have more ministry than I have money. I cannot pay the bills or meet payroll. My mailbox becomes flooded with shutoff notices, my phone rings with angry property owners demanding their money.

I have repeated this scenario many times, but because of my foolishness, God has used me to make an impact that will last long beyond my life. When I am dead, buried, and forgotten, the fruit of my imprudence will still be ripe with life-change for addicts, hot food for the hungry, shelter for the homeless, and the preaching of the Gospel to the poor.

One day during our first startup, my wife asked me why starting a mission had to be so hard. I told her that if it were easy, someone else would have already done it. She never asks me that question anymore; she knows that our commitment and calling come with a price.

Recently I heard someone pray this prayer over a crowd of people:

In the name of Jesus, I pray these blessings on those standing before me. I pray that you will bless them with plenty of money and prosperity, with good health, that you would meet all their needs, heal all their relationships, and bring great joy into each of their lives.

I leaned over and whispered to my wife, "What a dull, boring life that would be." It would be a dreary life without high mountains to climb, failures to reverse, stress and resistance that requires unimaginable perseverance to overcome and impossible tasks that entail enormous faith and trust in God.

Following the path of surrender means you seek God's will for your life over your hopes and dreams. As God works to form Christ's image in you, over time, your dreams and God's design for you unite into one grand purpose for your life. This whole process will produce a greater hunger for Christ to have His way with you in every aspect of your life. Eventually, you will no longer be concerned about any dream or plan that conflicts with God's will for your life.

Today is the day for you to surrender. Your desire to change cannot take place without the conquest of your "self." Do not be afraid of surrender. For years, your only surrender was to your "self," with not much to show for it. For some of you, your relationships are in shambles; you cannot overcome your habits and addictions; you have tried to change, but it simply has not happened. Take your "self" to the God who knows you better than you know yourself, and surrender to him; lay it at the altar. "Lord, do with me as you please. I no longer belong to myself. I belong to you."

Free Materials to Help you
Win your Battle with Addiction
www.winningtheaddictionbattle.com

Part Five: Change University

After you surrender your life to Christ, you must begin the process of change. Let us begin with a basic overview that will help you begin this process. You can use this process for any life-change that you want to make.

If you are like most people, you have succeeded at making some changes in your life; but the big issues, the ones that matter most to you, have proved to be unmovable, resistant to all your efforts, strategies, and plans to overcome them. You are stuck.

Most people are unhappy about something in their lives. People want to change their:

- Weight or health
- Financial situation
- Jobs
- Character
- Romantic state
- Future

Some of you may find yourselves in situations that threaten your survival and future if you do not take immediate steps to eradicate them from your life. Work on these first:

- Addiction
- Self-destructive habits
- Criminal justice issues
- Dangerous behavior

Why is it that some people seem to make a successful transition into a new life while others remain trapped in their current condition, unable to move forward?

If you want change to take place in your life, you must decide that your habit, character issue, addiction, or present circumstance is no longer acceptable. Get out a piece of paper, and write down your answers to the following questions:

- What is the situation, habit, character issue, or circumstance you would like to change?
- Why do you want to change it?
- Has your situation or issue caused harm or difficulties in your life? If so, what are they?
- What will happen to you or others close to you if you allow your present condition to continue?
- What are the benefits you and others around you will experience if you succeed in your journey for personal change?

Once you have answered these questions, you must make your decision. You must decide if the benefits of change outweigh the consequences of not changing. If they do, then proceed to the second step.

You must spell out what your change will look like in your life.

Get out another sheet of paper. Write down your goal. You must know what you are trying to achieve and what it will look like once you attain it. Once you set a goal, you will have a standard by which you can measure your progress. A goal will also provide you with encouragement when you are tempted to quit.

When you know what you are trying to accomplish, it becomes easier to formulate a plan for making a particular change happen in your life. It is not enough to want to change your present condition; you also need to know your destination. Without a goal, you just drift. Drifting is a guarantee that you will end up at a place that you did not choose.

Once you have written your goal on a sheet of paper, make copies of it. Place a copy on your refrigerator, bathroom mirror, computer screen, and any other place where you can regularly see it. Never take your eye off the goal. You must focus on what you are trying to achieve.

Make a plan.

As the saying goes, without a plan for success, you have a plan for failure. Here is what you must do to create a successful plan:

- Talk to other people who have succeeded in making the change or changes you are trying to make. If you do not know someone that can help you, find a website or book that deals with your problem. There are plenty of resources available for you. You are not alone. You do not have to start from scratch.
- Write the plan down, detailing step-by-step your plan for success.
- Make a checklist of activities in your plan that you must follow each day, week, and month. Follow it consistently.

Once you have made your plan, begin to implement it immediately. Read it daily to help you stay on track.

You must be willing to do, within moral and healthy boundaries, whatever it takes to make the necessary change(s) in your life.

Most people do not change because they are unwilling to pay the price, endure the hardships, and implement personal disciplines that are a vital part of the change process. Once you have decided that change is the best option for your future, you must be willing to tough it out as you experience new and difficult trials that are necessary for achieving your new life.

Here are some things to consider:

- The price for making changes in your life is less than the price for not changing.
- The process of change is temporary; the results of change will last the rest of your life.
- Failure is only fleeting if you get back on your feet and try again.

- The difficulties you encounter during your journey of change are the vital ingredients necessary for that change to happen.

Some things are impossible to change, but the things that bring real happiness and contentment can occur if you are willing to make the effort. Tomorrow is a horrible day to start. Tomorrow always becomes today and, thus, never happens. As soon as you finish reading this chapter, you should begin immediately.

Also, do not forget God. He cares for you. Enlist his help in this process. With his assistance comes strength for the journey.

God uses the particulars of your life as a training field for your future. Once you surrender to him, he is always in the background using the everyday occurrences of your life as tools of transformation.

In the next five chapters, I detail for you the different methods God uses to change your life. Understanding God's methods will help you not be discouraged or tempted to give up during your most difficult moments.

Here is a list of the topics we will discuss:

- Changing your thinking
- Developing a vision for your life
- The importance of time
- The critical nature of relationships
- Personal training for godliness

I attended college to prepare me for a life of ministry. My exposure to new ideas and people made a lasting impression on my life. Even today, years later, those experiences still influence my worldview.

In one sense, all of life is like a university. God is using your setbacks, successes, relationships, and other experiences to change your thinking, vision for the future, and character. Life is your classroom.

You can choose to waste your experiences and learn nothing from them. Of course, just like when you fail a class in college, you must repeat those experiences as many times as it takes to learn the right lessons for living a meaningful life. Usually, the second time is much harder than the first.

Get started. Class is in session.

Visit my website for free materials to help you
Win Your Battle with Addiction

www.winningtheaddictionbattle.com

Your Thinking Needs to Change

> *"I appeal to you therefore, brothers, by the mercies of God, to present your bodies as a living sacrifice, holy and acceptable to God, which is your spiritual worship. Do not be conformed to this world, but be transformed by the renewal of your mind, that by testing you may discern what is the will of God, what is good and acceptable and perfect."*
> (Romans 12:1-2, ESV)

Several years ago, one of the men in my residential program asked me if I had a few moments to talk. He seemed nervous. Despite his nervousness, he was determined to tell me what was on his mind. After a few moments, he blurted, "Don't mess with my mind. I can stand the chores and the other stuff we do. Just don't mess with my mind."

I felt sadness and concern. I responded, "Your addiction is not the cause of your problems. It is just a symptom of what is wrong with your thought processes. Unless we can help you change the way you think, we cannot help you recover from drugs." Within a few days, he disappeared. As of this writing, addiction is still in control of his life.

Surrender Is the Catalyst That Produces a Change in Our Thinking

In the previous chapters, I told you that change is the result of a surrendered life. Surrender is the channel that allows change to take place in your thinking, thereby wresting you from structures and worldviews that are not in harmony with the character of God. Without surrender, your thinking will remain mired in spent concepts that lead to self-destruction, broken relationships, and ingrained habits and addictions that exert absolute power over your destiny.

In the Scripture passage you just read, you read that a transformed mind is vital and necessary for determining and understanding the will of God. The problem with an untransformed mind is its inability to think clearly about what steps to take to bring about change in that person's life. In I Corinthians we read, "The natural person does not accept the things of the Spirit of God, for they are folly to him, and he is not able to understand them because they are spiritually discerned. " (I Corinthians 2:14, ESV)

Laying your life on the altar is the ultimate form of trust that a person can give to God. Surrender is an expression of your willingness to relinquish any person, place or thing that stands between you and God. This act of sacrifice is your acknowledgment that without God, life is senseless, without meaning. It is an expression of your dependency and trust, a belief that God has your back and that the best outcome for your life occurs when you surrender to Him. It signifies your recognition that you do not always know what is best for you, that sometimes your wisest perspective and understanding is inadequate for the obstacles you face on a daily basis.

That is why surrender is spiritual and not just physical or intellectual. It is a spiritual act of worship because it clears the self-will that blocks the flow of the Holy Spirit in your life. As the Spirit of God flows into your life, literally, the way you think begins to change.

Faulty Thinking Is the Root of Failure

Wrong thinking is the root of an immoral character, the herald of self-destruction, the cause of your endless cycle of relapse and disgrace. It is a perspective that traps you in addiction, places you in a destiny of failure, and imprisons you in behavior patterns that are beyond your escape. Faulty thinking is the way of a fool. Foolish thinking does not limit itself to the ignorant and uninformed. It is also the throne of the genius and powerful. You need only watch the news to know the truth of this statement.

The problem with faulty thinking is that it obstructs your ability to think clearly about a matter, or to know that your thinking is flawed. Your perspectives seem reasonable and right to you, indisputable, beyond question. In the drug culture, it is called "stinking thinking."

I remember sitting in a large waiting room filled with convicted felons on probation, each waiting to meet with his or her probation officer. I was with one of the men in my program, a man also on probation. I did not stand out as an authority figure because I wore jeans and a sweater, just like most of the other men and women in the room.

As I listened to their conversations, I could hardly believe what I was hearing. Work was for suckers. Upstanding citizens were fools. If you are smart, crime does pay. Punishment for a crime was wrong. It seemed to me that the whole world was upside down. Right was wrong; wrong was right.

The men and women sitting in that room were out of harmony in their thinking with the mainstream of society. If I had suggested to them they were wrong in their observations, and their conclusions concerning reality were wrong, they would conclude that I was the fool, a sucker, maybe someone they could manipulate for their benefit.

In many ways, we are just like those men and women who sat in that room. We are blind, but think we see; we are confused but think we understand; we are not in control but believe we are in charge. It is because of this tangled web of self-deceit, our inability to think on a spiritual level, that all efforts to change ultimately falter. We dream of living on a higher plane but are stuck, unable to rise beyond our current level.

Perhaps you have heard the hymn called "Amazing Grace." John Newton, a former slave trader, wrote the song after his conversion to Christianity. Here is the first verse:

> Amazing Grace, how sweet the sound,
> That saved a wretch like me,
> I once was lost but now am found,
> Was blind, but now, I see.

Changing Your Thinking Is a Product of Time Spent With God

Changing the way you think is a result of a relationship with God and time. It cannot happen overnight. Surrender is the soil that enables the work of the Holy Spirit in your life. Over time, as you surrender repeatedly, God's presence in your life transforms your thinking and creates an entirely new dynamic that changes your personal world and gives you victory over entrenched habits and sins.

The problem with much of your thinking is one of sources and influences. Your friends you spend time with, the shows you watch on television, the books you read, the hurts and pains, the setbacks and failures, the successes and triumphs all exert a powerful influence on your thought processes. They largely determine how you view and react to the events in your life. Sometimes life experiences can crush your dreams and beat you down so severely that you are unable to imagine a life beyond hopelessness and failure.

As you immerse yourself in Scripture, the Holy Spirit transforms your thinking and worldview, helping you to have victory over the most dangerous foe you will ever face—yourself. This process of immersion is essential for the repair of your thinking and behavior. Habits and flaws that seemed to be impregnable fortresses begin to crumble and fall, producing Christ-like behavior, a gradual manifestation of the fruit of the Spirit in your life.

Biblical Thinking Will Transform Your Perspectives on Life

The Apostle Paul wrote the following words to the church at Philippi:

"I rejoiced in the Lord greatly that now at length you have revived your concern for me. You were indeed concerned for me, but you had no opportunity. Not that I am speaking of being in need, for I have learned in whatever situation I am to be content. I know how to be brought low, and I know how to abound in any and every circumstance, I have learned the secret of facing plenty and hunger, abundance and need. I can do all things through him who

> *strengthens me."*
> (Philippians 4:10-13, ESV)

How you react to your daily experiences, the things that can make or break you, are largely a matter of your perspective or worldview. For instance, sometimes the sheer volume of stressful situations you regularly encounter can overwhelm you. You feel hemmed in, unable to function.

Your thought processes and perspectives greatly sway your reaction to stress. For some, stress is a destructive force they must avoid at all cost. Others find stress to be energizing, a natural byproduct of living a significant life.

Regardless of your view, stress is a fact of modern life. We stress over our schedules, the traffic, our work, our families, our finances, what other people think of us, our weight, our clothing, and the list continues, almost beyond counting. To combat stress we exercise, take prescription medication, abuse drugs, get drunk, take vacations, go to therapy, yell, scream, run, accuse, self-destruct, and withdraw from friends and family. If we are unable to manage stress, we may even wreck our lives.

If anyone knew about pressure, it would be the Apostle Paul. For Paul, stress was a daily confidante, an intimate acquaintance. It was not something he avoided, as he would some sort of plague. He saw stress as a normal consequence of a meaningful life.

Many of you, to reduce the stress in your life, attempt to adjust your daily activities in ways that help you avoid as much stress as possible. You dodge stressful people, look for less stressful jobs, avoid taking risks, and attempt to reduce your responsibilities. Sometimes, you get counseling to find balance in your life, to bring order out of the chaos of daily living.

Suppose you were successful in eliminating all stress from your life. A life without stress would be dull and boring, without challenge and risk. Without stress, your character would be stifled, lacking internal strength and fortitude. You would end up living the life of a coward, afraid of confrontation, unwilling to venture down any path that might upset the serenity of your stress-free life. In other words, your life would not count for much, because it would be without impact, barely making a ripple in the sea of humanity.

There is a common saying among Christians that people use to bring comfort to someone going through a crisis or a time of unbearable hardship. They say, "God wouldn't allow anything to come into your life that is more than you can bear." In other words, many people believe they can manage everything that comes into their lives; otherwise, God would not allow it to occur. If we could control our lives, why would we need God?

Look at the life of the Apostle Paul. Stress greeted him around every corner, a result of constant conflicts, setbacks, disappointments, and failures. His was a life of tension and pressure that was beyond even his ability to tolerate. It was a life lived beyond the limits of human endurance.

In II Corinthians, Paul said,

"We do not want you to be uninformed, brothers and sisters, about the troubles we experienced in the province of Asia. We were under great pressure, far beyond our ability to endure, so that we despaired of life itself. Indeed, we felt we had received the sentence of death. But this happened that we might not rely on ourselves but on God, who raises the dead."
II Corinthians 1:8-9 (NIV)

Paul just could not endure the conditions he was facing. By this, he meant that he lacked sufficient strength to face and overcome the challenges that confronted his life. Without help, he knew he was finished.

When Paul said that he had learned the secret of contentment in all circumstances, he was not talking about a life free of problems and challenges. Contentment did not mean that he was satisfied with the status quo, accepting without resistance whatever life threw at him. Paul was a warrior, a world-changer, someone who upset the established order.

For Paul, contentment was not rooted in external circumstances, abundant provision, or the absence of conflict; instead, his contentment was a result of his faith, based on experience, that God always had Paul's best interest at heart. Whatever happened to Paul, good or bad, could never overpower the power of God, nor prevent God's purpose from finding its fulfillment in his life. His contentment was faith in the goodness of God and His unlimited love and mercy.

When Paul said, "I can do all things through him who strengthens me," he never meant that God had turned him into Superman, able to leap tall buildings in a single bound. No, he meant that because of his faith in God, he could meet any challenge, any setback, and even any success with the assurance that no matter what the outcome, God was on his side.

Paul was able to live an immensely impactful life that changed the world because of his faith in God. When he said, "I have learned the secret," he meant that his thinking had changed concerning the meaning of his life experiences. He realized that all things in his life, whether directly caused by God or Paul's actions, were tools that God was using to make vital transformations in his life.

Faulty thinking causes us to react wrongly, or draw incorrect conclusions when faced with the constant hammering and flow of life. Even when confronted by positive experiences, faulty thinking can teach us the wrong lessons, resulting in misfortune at some future date.

Paul said that he had learned the secret of contentment. Since he had to learn to be content, then at some past point in life, just like you and me, he, too, was a victim of his thinking. It was a process.

Perhaps today you are overwhelmed with stress, fear, and discouragement. Your most intimate friend is your worry. It is your constant companion. Your emotions are destroying your quality of life and robbing you of your joy. Glumly, you wonder, will it ever end?

I cannot promise you your situation will ever get better. I do not know if your deliverance is just around the corner. I hope things will get better for you, but things may even get worse. From reading the Scriptures, I know Paul's situation never changed or got better. It continued until his execution by the Roman government.

Paul's situation did not change, but Paul changed. He learned how to face the growing onslaught of destruction and pain that ripped apart the serenity of his life. Inwardly, as he matured and became more like Christ, he began to appreciate the larger perspective of God's work in him. His life overflowed with meaning and purpose because God was hard at work forming in him the image of Christ.

With God's help, just like Paul, you can learn the secret of being content, of trusting God despite your circumstances. You can do all things through Christ. His strength will make a way for you out of the darkness. Ask him for help to continue trusting him. Your emotions lie when they tell you that God has abandoned you. He has never ceased working in your life.

When the way you think changes, your outward life is changed. Fortunately, God uses his Word and your relationship with him to effect that transformation. His Holy Spirit can powerfully work in your life and transform your thinking. This change will reveal itself in your character and relationships. The fruit of the Spirit will begin to distinguish itself in your life; you become more like Christ and less like your old self.

Do not be afraid to think biblically. As you read and meditate on the Scriptures, ask God to line up your thought processes with what you are reading. Over time, your thinking will change, creating a completely new world for your life and significantly enriching your relationships and emotional health. Start today.

Free Materials to Help you
Win your Battle with Addiction
www.winningtheaddictionbattle.com

Developing a Vision for Change

"So we do not lose heart. Though our outer self is wasting away, our inner self is being renewed day by day. For this light momentary affliction is preparing for us an eternal weight of glory beyond all comparison, as we look not to the things that are seen but to the things that are unseen. For the things that are seen are transient, but the things that are unseen are eternal."
(II Corinthians 4:16-18, ESV)

Tammy lost heart. All she could see was the broken windows, the smashed plumbing fixtures, the missing pipes, the gaping holes in the walls, and the mountains of trash. As she looked at the mess, her bottom lip began to quiver; a tear rolled down her face. "I don't want to live here," she cried.

We were in Bridgeport, Connecticut, starting our first mission. The house was in one of the most dangerous neighborhoods in the city. The location was not the problem. We already lived in the same neighborhood. The problem was the house. She could not envision that shell of a house becoming a home for our family.

"But, Baby, can't you see? Look. Luis can have his own room. So can Daniel, Angelina, Anais, and Anna. Look at the size of this kitchen. It even has a huge pantry. The dining room will hold an enormous table, big enough for the whole family and even a few friends. Look how large the living room is. There is even space for a family room. I know it does not look like much, but, Baby, it's our dream house." We never lived in that house. She could not see what I saw.

Difficulties, setbacks, and failures are the stuff of life. We struggle not to quit, to keep moving forward. Sometimes it seems as though our suffering is senseless, without meaning, with no hope of relief. Our pain seems beyond explanation, as though God no longer cares about us. We feel abandoned, left to our own devices, escape impossible.

Sometimes, it is hard to understand God's methods. If only we could figure out what God was doing. If we could somehow understand the purpose of our predicament, then we could persevere, not forsake our calling. If only we could see what God sees, then we could hang tough, keep on fighting, never surrender.

The Apostle Paul understood suffering. Hardship and setbacks were his constant companions as he lived and fulfilled the call God had on his life. It seemed as though trouble knew his name and even his address; it regularly knocked on his door. Imprisonment, stonings and beatings, arrests, riots, narrow escapes, shipwrecks, and even snakebite was on his resume, descriptions of the price he paid for his faith. Some of his friends betrayed him. Other Christians slandered his reputation. Chased from one city to another, his enemies hounded him, seeking his destruction. If you look closely at his writings, you will see hints of depression and the temptation to quit.

In the midst of all of this, he said, ". . . we do not lose heart." What was his secret? What made him press on, not quit, and never give up? In these same verses, he called these problems "light momentary affliction." Any one of his problems would have destroyed most of us.

For us, a false statement, a minor setback, or a simple inconvenience can bring us to the brink of despair. We wallow in self-pity, cry about our misfortune, and plot our revenge. It is as though our nerves are exposed, not protected, sensitive to the slightest touch. We do not seem to have an inner toughness to help navigate the problems confronting our lives. Why was Paul able to endure such difficult emotional and physical trials?

Paul had vision. His problems were "light and momentary" because he saw them from the perspective of eternity. When the authorities stoned or beat him, when they opened his flesh with the lash, the pain was real. It hurt. He did not enjoy it. Despite all the turmoil and suffering he experienced, he knew his hardships would end, that God would raise him up and wipe the tears from his face. Eternity would be the end of pain, a place of reunion with loved ones, mountains of joy, forever in the presence of God.

Paul's vision for his life was big. Many of us do have a vision, but it is too small to make much of a difference in the daily routine of our lives. It does not inspire us to make great sacrifices, to stomach unpleasant and unimaginable hardship, to risk significant loss for colossal gain, and to interpret all of life from the perspective of our vision. Our vision of God is too small, too diluted, and too weak.

A small vision is rooted in a theology that believes in absolute certainty for all of life. We never attempt anything great for God unless we secure financing in advance, doors are wide open, and everything falls into place. We are not like Paul, who knocked on doors all over Asia Minor, sure in his calling, not so sure where. He did not wait for perfect circumstances, for everything to be in place. He was not afraid of failure.

We have masked our fear of failure in pious clichés that excuse our lack of nerve. "Failure will bring dishonor to God," we say. Somehow, we have come to believe that faith in Christ turns us into super humans, men and women who never fail or go belly up and wreck themselves. This belief weakens us.

What Does Vision Have to Do With Change?

Vision strengthens you and steels you for the daily tasks and problems you encounter as you journey through life. Vision makes it possible to find significance in your most trying circumstances. Like the soldier who sacrifices his/her life for his/her country, you interpret your life through the prism of your vision. Because of your eternal perspective: "We do not lose heart."

My mission startup in Gary, Indiana, was one of the most challenging endeavors of my life. It teetered on the precipice of disaster from its inception. In my struggle to bring it to maturity, I was plunged deeply into debt, lost credibility with some friends and supporters, and had to beg other donors for support to keep the doors open. Close friends encouraged me to walk away from it and begin the process of rebuilding my life.

During the midst of all these trials, our residential program almost collapsed under the weight of a plague of bedbugs. We had to spend over $15,000 to eradicate the problem. Most of the men in the program fled the coop. For almost six months, the men in our program were part of the food chain. Who could blame them?

Hearing about our troubles, one of our supporters invited me to meet with him in his office to discuss the situation at the mission. At least six other individuals joined the discussion. Instead of helping with our financial need, he humiliated me in front of everyone else at the meeting. His behavior made me feel embarrassed.

After the meeting, I described to my wife the details of the meeting. She asked, "How can you let him keep doing that to you? Why?" My response: "I can't let my pride stand in the way of successfully launching this mission. I know there are only a few brave souls left at the mission. Still, in the future, this mission will help thousands of men and women trapped in addiction get their lives back. In the future, thousands upon thousands of men, women, and children will get a hot meal at the mission, an act of compassion that just might be a turning point in their lives. I cannot let my pride prevent this from happening. If I quit, I will let down thousands of needy people who are counting on me not to quit. I will not let them down."

Vision gives us the backbone to remain true to our convictions. Without vision, difficulties may wear us down and cause us to succumb to our baser nature. A lack of vision stampedes us from the battlefield, destroys our will to persevere, and wrecks our moral foundation during times of distress and hurt.

Without Vision, Failure Is an Option

Recently I began a strict regimen of physical exercise and diet. It is not the first diet and exercise program I have attempted. I often tell people that I have lost over a thousand pounds—the same twenty pounds over-and-over again. Ever since my early forties, I have been on at least a dozen diets.

I began each one filled with enthusiasm and anticipation: This time I am going to succeed. Some of my diets only lasted a few days. I was on the Akins Diet for almost three years. Most of the diets lasted for about six months. Eventually, I would capitulate to McDonald's and Kentucky Fried Chicken, the real rulers of my life.

Looking thinner and fitting back into some of my clothing was not a big enough vision to motivate me to succeed. At some point in time, satisfying my immediate hunger became more important than thinness. Am I just plain weak, without sufficient willpower to maintain a proper weight for my height? Perhaps thinness is an inadequate vision to sustain me through the struggles and temptations to quit that are a part of a diet and exercise program?

Apparently, I need a bigger reason than thinness for losing weight. Up until now, I have failed to stay on every diet I have attempted. The same cycle repeats itself every time I try to lose weight, with each cycle ending in disappointment. I could blame the diet, thus evading personal responsibility. "It's not my fault" is a great place to take refuge. It makes it easier for me to accept failure as an option. Maybe I need to formulate a vision larger than thinness to fortify me for my weight-loss journey, giving me a reason not to succumb to my hunger.

Your Vision Must Be God-Inspired

A bigger vision for your life must be rooted in your relationship with God. God has the power to defeat your addiction or bad behavior and make your vision for your life materialize. A vision not bathed with the power of God is meaningless and futile. It is too small to provide you with the necessary sticking power for accomplishing the purpose of your life.

The supreme vision for your life and mine must flow from God's ultimate purpose for us. In Romans 8:29 (The Message Bible) we read, "God knew what he was doing from the very beginning. He decided from the outset to shape the lives of those who love him along the same lines as the life of his Son."

Since we know that Christ-likeness is God's purpose for our lives, we can chart a vision connected to that purpose. All the obligations in the Scripture flow from Christ-likeness. Therefore, any vision we construct must be consistent with that purpose.

For example, evangelism is at the very heart of God's love for the world. If our vision is to reach our community with the Gospel, our methods and strategies will be consistent with Christ-like behavior. Our purpose is the foundation of our vision. Christ-like motives that seek to bring honor to God are the guiding principles for our vision. The vision cannot be about the self-promotion of the evangelist, church or evangelistic organization; instead, the focus is on the glory of God.

I wish I could say that I have always been Christ-like in my motives and behavior. As I look back over my life, there were many times when my behavior was anything but Christ-like, and my motivations were more about Jim Watson than bringing honor to God.

So often, pride and unholy ambition drove my vision instead of the glory of God. I allowed nothing to get in the way of my success. Sometimes others had to pay the price for my success, especially my wife and family.

Vision without Christ-likeness wreaks havoc on organizations, relationships, marriages, and reputations. When your vision comes before purpose, self-sufficiency and the will to succeed, become the driving forces behind the vision. Ultimately, the culmination of the vision becomes a monument to the visionary leader and his followers.

If vision does not flow from Christ-likeness, then it is susceptible to corruption by the ebb and flow of success and failure. Christ-likeness keeps our motives in check, pride from consuming our successes and personal and institutional power regulated by humility and dependency on God.

Christ-likeness is a product of your relationship with God. The Scriptures are the primary source for your relationship with God. Secondary sources of interaction are circumstances and events in your life, the input of godly men and women, and the still, small voice that speaks to you in your prayers and meditations.

The Spirit of God uses all these interactions to help you formulate a vision for your life. Christ-likeness is the plumb line for measuring your vision. Consequently, as you grow in Christ, you must continuously modify your vision to accommodate your growing maturity and Christ-likeness.

The purpose of your life is Christ-likeness. Your vision is the mission that God has called you to live out in this world. Christ-likeness fills that vision with godliness and ultimately brings glory to God. Bringing glory to God is the supreme goal of your vision and life.

All Christians should live Christ-like lives. It is our calling. Make that calling the highest priority of your life. Seek to live a life that brings glory to God. Ask God to give you a vision for your life. Build that vision on the foundation of Christ-likeness. A vision that originates from godliness rests on a solid footing and brings glory to God regardless of its success or failure. Do not settle for a small vision. Ask God for a vision that challenges you to be bigger than you are.

If you have a vision for your life, sacrifice for the fulfillment of that vision is not an aberration or mistake, but a necessary component of success. Start looking at God's big picture for your life. Without that picture, you will sink in the bog of every trouble and setback. Instead, be like Caleb. He went to the high country, chasing down giants. He had vision. Do you have a vision?

Free Materials to Help you
Win your Battle with Addiction
www.winningtheaddictionbattle.com

Relationships Can Help You Change

The first few years of my marriage were tough. I was thirty-four years old on the day of our wedding. I was certain that I was a great catch for Tammy. Having been single for so long, with no one to contradict my belief in my personal goodness, what could I think otherwise? What is not to love?

It did not take long for our relationship to shake my view of myself. It was easy to be a great person when I was all alone. When I added Tammy to the equation, my theory about me came under severe testing. I did not understand why she was always crying. I was just trying to enlighten her with my words of wisdom. I figured there must be something wrong with her.

It finally came to a head one day during one of our discussions about some of her issues and shortcomings. "But what about your issues?" she yelled. I thought her frustration and anger were unwarranted. After all, I was just trying to help her. "I know all about my issues. I have one or two faults. I see what they are. I am working on them. Let us get back to you. Don't try to change the subject." She did not react well.

Over time, I began to understand that many of the problems in our marriage were my fault. I was to blame. Without my relationship with Tammy, I never would have realized how proud and vain I was. In isolation, we all look virtuous to ourselves.

You will never reach your potential unless you have other people in your life who know you well enough to speak the truth to you. Left to yourself, you become stagnant, stuck, and even directionless. When you are the major influence in your life, you shrink and become small, a victim of your delusions concerning your personal goodness and importance. Your aloneness produces destructive pride.

Relationships Are Essential for Change to Take Place in Your Life

God did not create you to be alone. God created you to be in a relationship with Him and with other people. So much of the instruction in the Scriptures is about how you relate to others. For instance, in Romans 12:15-16 (ESV), we read,

> "Rejoice with those who rejoice, weep with those who weep. Live in harmony with one another. Do not be haughty, but associate with the lowly. Never be wise in your own sight."

How can you rejoice and weep with those who are celebrating and mourning without being in a relationship with them? The act of grieving with someone who is hurting or delighting in the success or happiness of someone else moves you beyond the realm of selfishness and into biblical love. Love is the true measure of your faith.

Isolation allows you to continue living life as you please, without consideration of your impact on others. You can be bad-tempered and unattractive, oblivious to the hurt of others and indifferent to the plight of the less fortunate.

How do relationships change you? What difference can it make in your life?

Relationships are a powerful tool God uses to transform you into his image. It is amazing how so many men and women can trace their personal success to the influence of a parent, teacher, or friend. Interaction with others always produces change, some good and some bad.

Growth takes place when you choose to respond to a person's actions or words in a manner that is consistent with biblical principles. Your interactions with other people teach you many of the lessons you need for successful living. You cannot always control someone else's behavior, but you can learn to control your reaction to their conduct.

God can use even bad relationships to accomplish his purpose for your life. When you forgive someone who has terribly wronged you, you are overcoming your propensity to react emotionally in a destructive manner. In reality, your act of forgiveness is surrender to the higher calling of God for your life. When you respond to someone's injustice or flagrant disregard for your feelings in a manner consistent with God's character, you become more Christ-like. You grow.

Church Is a Great Place to Start

Despite all the justifiable criticisms of the church, the church is still God's method for growing Christians and reaching the world through evangelism and compassion. You will not find Christ-like men and women in the church. Instead, you will find men and women who are in the process of becoming more like Christ. Thrown in for good measure, you will also find individuals who are the sons and daughters of Satan. The Bible calls them tares.

The church is the perfect setting for spiritual growth and pooling resources to reach the world for Christ. At church, you will find like-minded people who will accompany you on your journey of faith. You will find mentors and spiritual directors who can provide you with guidance and a personal example of living the Christian life. Your pastor will teach you how to live by his preaching and his life. Together, as a church, you will affect your community and the world.

Mature Christian will influence, strengthen, and inspire you to live a great and godly life. You will do life together and be better for it. Fellow Christians will walk with you during the hard times. When the world forsakes you, they will not abandon you.

As you interact and relate with others by exercising compassion, mercy, and hope, God is preparing you for a life of significance, a life beyond measure. You are growing, maturing, and changing. You are becoming more like Christ.

Their Influence Changed John's Life

The first time I met John, he was in his early thirties. He came to my mission in Roanoke Rapids, North Carolina, looking for a bed. He had been living out on the streets, imprisoned and wrecked by his addiction to alcohol. He was not impressive as a person.

The only thing John was interested in doing was reserving a bed for later on that evening. Several months later, he confessed to me that he had enough money in his pocket that day to buy a cheap bottle of wine. He wanted to make sure that he had a bed to sleep in after he finished off the bottle. I told him that we did not take reservations. If he wanted our help, he would have to join the program immediately. Reluctantly, he agreed.

That night at our mission, as was our custom, we had a chapel service for all the residents of the mission. John pitched a fit. No way was he going to allow us to force him to attend a religious service. However, when confronted with the possibility of losing his bed, he relented.

That night was a point of change in John's life. At the end of the service, I offered all those in attendance an opportunity to surrender their lives to Christ. John came to the altar and made that surrender. He was never the same again.

At first, his growth as a Christian was not impressive. At night, he would steal food from the refrigerator used by the men in the program to store their snacks. Frustrated by the loss of their food, the men decided to trap him by putting a laxative in the chocolate milk. John spent most of the next day on the toilet located just outside of my office. Several months later, the men confessed to me what they had done.

When cornered, John would lie to cover up his wrongdoing. One day, I noticed that the top edge of the box on our brand-new truck had sustained some damage. Since John was the driver, I asked him what happened. He told me that it came like that from the factory. Later I learned that while he was attempting to beat a train at the crossing guard, the guard came down on the truck and flattened that corner.

After John had been at the mission for several months, a couple of men from one of the local churches approached me about the possibility of mentoring John. I readily agreed. I was excited about this opportunity for John.

Those men exerted an enormous influence on John. Not only did they pick him up every week for church services, but they also took him out to eat and spent time with him. I believe their influence on John's life far exceeded my own. They were God's instruments of change in John's life. The last I heard of John, he was married with a family, heading up a mission he had founded to reach men just like him.

Find Yourself a Mentor

I have had many mentors in my life. They were men who believed in me and saw something in me that most other people failed to see. They patiently guided me, offering advice and encouragement when I needed it and provided inspiration for me to fulfill God's call for my life. Looking back, I am so grateful for the guidance of Reverend Paul Fleming, Reverend Frank Perry, and Dr. John Carlton, men who exerted an immeasurable influence on my life. Even now, I am searching for someone to help guide me through the next season of my life.

You need a mentor too. Without one, you will not reach your full potential. Find one today.

Become a Mentor

No matter where you are in your life, you can always find someone who needs you to help them reach their potential. Your experiences, both positive and negative, have taught you things that will benefit others who are desperately in need of guidance. Become a mentor.

Conclusion

You need help to grow spiritually and defeat your addiction. To think that you do not need guidance and motivation from others to reach your potential is detrimental to your future success. In reality, it is suicidal.

Without others, your life will become like Scrooge in Dickens's Christmas Carol. You end up never reaching your potential. You waste your life. Do life with others. Start today.

Time is on Your Side

His name was Ricky. Ricky was a young man in his late twenties with a very checkered past. He had been in trouble with the authorities since his early teens. Addiction, robbery, violence and some lesser crimes were all a part of his resume.

When he told me about his upbringing, his tales of abuse and neglect seemed consistent with his current lifestyle. Ricky was a three-time loser, a victim of his self-destructive behavior. His future looked bleak and foreboding. Without a significant change in his outlook and conduct, he was destined to live a life of misery, be constantly on the run from the law, and continue barreling towards an early encounter with death.

Eventually, Ricky's addiction so scrambled his life that he ended up homeless on the streets, with no place to go and without any friends or family to turn to for help. Hearing about our program, Ricky called me up on the phone to see if he could join our life-change program.

Our program was a faith-based, one-year program, designed to help a man get his life back on track and become a productive member of society. Out of options, Ricky agreed to join the program with all its rules and restrictions.

The next thirty days were anything but easy for Ricky. His basic code of conduct was conflict and rebellion. It was somewhat of a miracle that he lasted as long as he did. On his thirtieth day, he informed me that he was ready to leave. "I've been clean from drugs for thirty days. Thirty days is the longest I have been clean since I started using drugs in my early teens. I'm cured."

That afternoon he left the program. We never saw Ricky again. The last we heard of him, the police were after him for armed robbery.

It is easy to be critical of Ricky for not devoting enough time to allow the changes in his life to take hold. He should have known that a lifetime of bad thinking was not reversible in just a few short weeks. In his eagerness to get on with the rest of his life, he neglected to lay a solid foundation that would see him through the temptations and troubles that are a part of every man or woman's life.

In his hurry to restart his life, he did not prepare himself for the responsibilities that come with freedom. Although we were able to see some changes in his outward behavior, he was still the same man who walked through our doors. Once he left our place, he was unable to navigate the struggles and worries of a drug-free environment.

In a sense, the process of becoming like Christ is the waiting and not quitting, the continuation of a disciplined life of prayer and meditation on God's Word despite our lack of progress and results. The only way to reverse our rebellion against God and ourselves is to embark on a schedule of consistent daily discipline over an extended period.

However, this does not happen overnight. If you are like most people, you are always in a hurry, desperate for God to get the job done as quickly as possible. He will get the job done. Quickly, though, is from God's perspective, not your own. He looks at a thousand years as simply one day. Despite all of your objections, pleading, and impatience, he is never in a hurry. Why do you expect God to accelerate the process of change in your life when he spent forty years training Moses for the supreme mission of his life? Are you better than Moses was?

A changed life is, in reality, the fruit of your daily relationship with God, of time devoted to hanging out with him on a regular basis. Busy people find comfort in the oft-repeated cliché that quality time in a relationship is more important than the quantity of time spent with someone. Perhaps that explains why most people fail to experience deep and meaningful relationships.

Time is one of God's primary tools for healing and transforming the damage that you have inflicted on yourself. As you read the Bible, it will become apparent to you that God is never in a hurry. He looks at your life from the perspective of eternity, always mindful of your need for preparation and seasoning before launching you on your life mission. To be God's man or woman is to have been equipped and prepared for the trial of time and circumstance.

Moses, a prince of Egypt, spent forty years in the desert caring for the sheep of his father-in-law before he was ready to meet his destiny. David's preparation for becoming the king of Israel meant living life on the run, in exile, in fear for his life, continually plagued by memories of prophecies unfulfilled. Paul, the man on fire for God, had to endure three years in the Arabian Desert and years of exile in Tarsus before Barnabas brought him to Antioch to work alongside him among the new believers. Even then, he needed several more years of seasoning before the church launched him on his first missionary journey.

For each of these men, the transformation in their lives did not occur in the twinkling of an eye. A change of direction can happen in a moment, but the overhaul of a person's character takes time. Conversion causes a dramatic change in our worldview and perspective, but only time can transform our thinking.

God, the master artist, uses the events and happenings of your life, over time, to paint the image of Christ in your personality and character.

As you experience the trial of discouragement and the ordinary tasks of everyday life, it often feels as though God has abandoned you, with little thought for your pain and hurt. Despite your feelings, in the center of your pain, God is busy accomplishing His will for you. Your pain may cause you to become impatient, to look for shortcuts and easier methods. It may even seem as though life has conspired against you to prevent you from achieving your cherished ambitions and goals.

When Jesus was on the cross, the mass of humanity was oblivious to his misery and agony. Even worse, a close companion betrayed him, and most of his dearest friends and confidants deserted him. More disheartening still, from the gloomy pit of the cross, shrouded in waves of loneliness, he cried out, "My God, My God, why have you forsaken me?" (Mark 15:34b, NIV) On the cross, he was all alone. As life slowly ebbed from his tortured body, each moment must have seemed like an eternity, a merciless reminder of God's desertion in the midst of His need.

Still, moments before he died, drained from his struggle with death, "Jesus called out with a loud voice, 'Father, into your hands I commit my spirit'." (Luke 23:46, NIV) As he breathed his final breath, his last words were words of trust. Despite all the evidence to the contrary, he still believed that his Father loved him and that his future was secure in his hands. He knew that God was always working, regardless of how desperate the situation seemed, to accomplish his will in his life.

In one sense, the slow-moving nature of the Spirit of God exercises your spiritual muscles, increasing your faith as you persevere over time, continue to believe, continue to trust, and never quit. Your walk with God is similar to the process of cooking food in a crock-pot. A crock-pot is a slow cooker that brings out the distinctness and flavor of each ingredient.

For years, whenever I attempted to make beef stew in a pot on the stove, the meat was always tough and gnarly, almost unfit to eat. Then I tried cooking the stew in a crock-pot, slowly, on low heat for about ten hours. I could cut the meat with a fork. It took longer to cook in the crock-pot, but it tasted better than the stew cooked at a raging boil on the stovetop.

Significant spiritual growth does not suddenly occur, as if by magic, in an instant. Over an extended period, your life simmers in the heat of God's Word, the events and circumstances that make up your life, and the loving action of the Holy Spirit, transforming you into a picture of the Christ, giving you a life of decency and influence.

Time is the incubator of your faith in God, the essential ingredient for change. It trains you to continue trusting God and to believe he is at work in your life despite the lack of outward evidence.

Time Spent with God Makes You More like Him

When my wife and I were first married, the gap between our similarities and differences was wide. I was serious about everything. I also had convictions about everything, such as what brand of dishwashing liquid we should use and where to locate the spices and canned goods. Tammy was serious about important things, but she did not sweat the small stuff. Moreover, she loved to laugh and have fun.

Over time, we have become more alike. I have learned to laugh and not take myself so seriously. I am better for the years I have spent with Tammy. My relationship with Tammy has changed me.

A relationship has the power to change you, sometimes for your benefit and sometimes to your detriment. Tammy is a positive force for change in my life. I love spending time, a lot of time, with her. The amount of time I spend with her is a reliable indicator of the value I place on our relationship. If I were always too busy to spend time with her, she could correctly conclude that our relationship was a low priority in my life.

If you are serious about changing your life, you must dedicate significant blocks of time towards deepening your relationship with God. Never forget that God is working in your life in the same way he worked in the lives of Moses, David, and Paul. It took time for God to do his work in their lives. It will take time for God to accomplish his purpose for you. Please do not surrender to discouragement and disappointment. Remember what Paul said in Romans 8:22-25 (The Message Bible):

"All around us we observe a pregnant creation. The difficult times of pain throughout the world are simply birth pangs. But it's not only around us; it's within us. The Spirit of God is arousing us within.

We're also feeling the birth pangs. Some sterile and barren bodies of ours are yearning for full deliverance. That is why waiting does not diminish us, any more than waiting diminishes a pregnant mother. We are enlarged in the waiting. We, of course, don't see what is enlarging us. But the longer we wait, the larger we become, and the more joyful our expectancy."

It takes time to build a foundation in your life that can withstand the shaking and chaos of dialing living. Time, or waiting, is the process that God uses to strengthen you for living a consequential life.

Continue to have hope for what God is doing in your life. Do not miss the most important things in your life. Time is your friend and not your enemy. He is working!

Free Materials to Help you
Win your Battle with Addiction
www.winningtheaddictionbattle.com

Train yourself to be Godly

"Rather train yourself for godliness...."
I Timothy 4:7 (ESV)

Most men and women live undisciplined lives, especially addicts. An unorganized life can only produce turmoil in your daily living, relationships, finances, and career. Without discipline, you will never beat your addiction and fulfill the ambitions you have for your life. An undisciplined life is a dream-killer.

Most men and women wait until they have a serious problem before they decide to do something about it. We wait until we get a little plump around the middle before we choose to switch to a more healthy diet. We wait until our kids get into trouble before we spend more time with them. We only seek help for our marriage when it is in danger of failing. We check into a rehab program after alcohol or drugs have destroyed our lives. The whole thought of discipline smacks of excessive regimentation, a lack of spontaneity in our lives.

Reasons for Our Dislike of Discipline

Our dislike for training has several root causes. For some of us, laziness is the culprit that continually gets in the way of our success or life-change. We are simply unwilling to do the hard work necessary to change the course of our lives and destiny.

For others, the busyness of life stands in the way of providing structure in our daily routine. A disciplined lifestyle is a "burden too far" we believe may lead to our collapse.

Even more common are those of us that have simply given up on ever changing. Our past failures have discouraged us from believing personal change is possible. "What's the use?" we say. "It's impossible for me to change. I have always been this way, and this is the way I will always be." We simply cannot see the benefits of a disciplined lifestyle.

As you know, I have spent many years working with men and women with drug and alcohol addictions. Many of the men and women I worked with seemed to be incapable of taking a long-term perspective in decisions regarding their futures. They lived for the moment, oblivious to the enduring consequences of their actions. For them, today is the only day that matters. Perhaps that describes you.

For most of you, addiction is only one of many things that trouble your life. Maybe you struggle with anger and lust, insatiable cravings for spreading gossip about friends and acquaintances, the need to criticize others, and a multitude of other unchristian behaviors.

Our experiences falsely teach us to be content with the current level of progress in our personal growth. Spiritual maturity becomes knowledge about the Bible and witnessing to others about the Gospel. Why anyone would ever respond to a message that is so powerless is beyond my comprehension.

Maybe you are looking for a quick fix that will produce instantaneous results. You want to change today and overcome habits that have taken a lifetime to plant their tentacles in your character and thinking. You have come to believe that if you just had the right information, a straightforward and easy formula or even a dramatic experience of the Holy Spirit, you could conquer any habit that causes harm. Maybe the problem is with your vision for your life. You have learned to settle for an unimportant life, a life that hardly matters. An inconsequential vision is hardly worth the effort.

Most athletes dream big. To accomplish their vision, they are willing to live highly disciplined lifestyles and sacrifice whatever is necessary to obtain their goals. They know they have to do more than just read all the books ever written on their sport; a training plan followed by action is necessary for them to reach their full potential as an athlete.

Godliness Is the Fruit of Discipline and the Work of the Holy Spirit

Much like training for an athletic event, you must train yourself to be godly. In other words, godliness does not happen by accident. It is the result of diligent and persistent effort, yet it is still a work of the Holy Spirit in your life.

How can both of these be true at the same time? Well, they are. Once you understand the relationship between training yourself to be godly and the Holy Spirit changing you from within, you will be on your way to becoming the man or woman God destined you to become.

Godliness training helps you defeat your addiction.

Why do you need to train? If godliness is the work of the Holy Spirit, why put so much effort into the process of becoming godly? Why not just sit still and let God make the changes? Unfortunately, letting go and letting God is nothing more than an empty cliché without any connection to the real world. In reality, you cannot just simply let go and let God.

You have spent a lifetime building a wall that protects you from any outside intrusion that may rock your personal world or challenge any of your deeply held beliefs. You are afraid of surrender and unable to trust God with many areas of your life. Your wall of protection is both high and wide.

Your wall of protection is the total of your life experiences. When someone hurts you, you add another brick to your wall to protect you from being hurt again. If a spouse or romantic friend cheats on you, your employer fires you, someone ridicules or laughs at you, a supposed friend gossips about you, you increase the height of your wall to prevent those actions from doing damage to you again. You also add bricks to the wall by your actions. The continued practice of sin in your daily life hardens your heart and increases the strength and thickness of your wall.

I started my first mission in a city called Bridgeport, Connecticut. I spent my first year in Bridgeport preaching and feeding in some of the city's most dangerous neighborhoods and drug-infested parks. My wife and I prepared meals in borrowed kitchens and served them out of the back of our old station wagon. Before we would feed, Tammy would sing a Gospel song, and I would preach a short evangelistic message.

Hundreds of people—gang members, prostitutes, and children—came to our street feedings. The sights and sounds of life and death in the inner city overwhelmed us. We saw children playing on playgrounds covered with broken wine bottles and empty syringes, drug dealers selling crack and heroin, addicts with needle marks all over their arms, and even a drive-by shooting.

Towards the end of our first year, I received a phone call from a couple that owned a rooming house right in the heart of where Tammy and I were doing our ministry. The owners had heard that we were looking for a building and were wondering if we might be interested in leasing their property.

What we did not know was that a street gang had started using their building for drug dealing and prostitution. The owners were desperate and afraid. Complicating the situation, the week before we moved in to the property another gang tried to wrestle control of the building from the first gang. The new gang machine-gunned the building, barely missing one of the female tenants. Although they shot up the place, they failed to oust the gang in control.

It did not take me long to figure out that if I wanted to use their building for ministry, it would be my responsibility to evict the gang from the building. I decided not to involve the police, figuring that ultimately their help would alienate those I wanted to reach with the Gospel. I must admit, the prospect of ejecting them from the building was very frightening to me.

The week before it was time for me to move into the building, I decided to pay the neighborhood a visit and get a feel for its environment. I watched from my parked car just down the street from the building. I saw drug dealers swap drugs for dollars, passing them into the hands of anxious addicts eager for a fix and prostitutes yelling at passing cars, like hawkers outside a pawnshop.

After I had been there for about fifteen minutes, one of the prostitutes crossed the street and approached me. She wanted to know if I was a cop. I told her I was a pastor, that I had rented their building and was planning to open a mission in it the following Sunday. She returned to the building.

A few minutes later, one of the drug dealers shouted at me from the other side of the street. He told me that if I attempted to enter the building, they would kill me. I believed him.

When I first became a Christian, I read a book called Fox's Book of Martyrs. The book detailed the stories of men and women that had endured great hardship and suffering. Because of their willingness to stand firm in their faith, they suffered severe persecution from both the church and state. Many of them experienced horrendous deaths. Their compelling testimonies and their willingness to lose all for the sake of Christ gripped my heart.

Initially, my new faith compelled me to surrender my life to Christ, to be willing, if necessary, to make the ultimate sacrifice, the loss of my life. Now my faith had aged, my circumstances changed with the addition of a wife and children.

Instead of relishing the possibility of death, I just wanted to run. The crisis and danger of this situation vividly demonstrated to me my fear of mortality. I was a coward. My faith in Christ, faith that should have prepared me for this battle, seemed to fail me.

Christian friends tried to comfort me by their assurances that God would not let anything bad happen to me. Anyone who has read the Bible knows that Christians can die doing God's will. It happens all the time.

My struggle continued for days. Things that I had taken for granted came into sharp focus—my love for my wife, watching my children grow into adults, flowers blooming, birds singing, hamburgers and French fries. I cried out to God for help.

It was at this crisis point that I remembered the words written by Jim Elliot in his journal; he penned them before he set out as a missionary to a tribe of headhunters in Ecuador. He wrote, "He is no fool, who gives what he cannot keep, to gain what he cannot lose." The headhunters he hoped to win to Christ speared Jim and his companions to death.

As I reflected on Jim's words and faith, my fear, though still present, surrendered to a higher calling. I realized that the loss of my life for the sake of Christ would become the entryway that led me to a place where pain ceased to exist, tears dried up, sickness subdued, and hope finds fulfillment. Feeling somewhat foolish because of my fear, I decided that trading my life for a future with God was a winning proposition. I made up my mind to go for it.

The day for taking possession of the building finally arrived. Before going over to the building, I held my wife in my arms for a very long time. I wondered if I would ever see her again on this side of the grave.

When I arrived at the building, I unlocked the front door and walked into the main room. Gang members and prostitutes were everywhere. Summoning up all the courage I could muster, I announced that the building was now the property of Bridgeport Rescue Mission. I told them all to leave. They left! At least, it seemed that way for the moment.

Several of the gang members barricaded themselves in a couple of the rooms in the back of the building. I was still certain that I was going to die; I demanded that they open the door and leave the building. They refused. Like a reincarnation of John Wayne, I kicked in the door. I am not a huge person. It hurt. They escaped out the window.

God Will Not Enter a Closed Door

You and I might kick open a door that prevents us from obtaining something we want. We do not want to take "No" for an answer. We might even intrude into a place without an invitation. God is not like us. He will not enter into an area of your life uninvited.

God will not work in any area of your life you have not surrendered to Him. Because you, like most other people, selfishly cling to ownership of particular areas of your life, certain dispositions, individual plans or dreams, God cannot, because of his very nature, shape the character of Christ in that part of your life. He will not use his power to overpower your will. That is the reason you still find it so difficult to forgive, defeat addiction, overcome your temper, or exhibit the fruit of the Spirit in your daily living.

Galatians 5:22-24 (ESV) says,

"But the fruit of the Spirit is love, joy, peace, patience, kindness, goodness, faithfulness, gentleness and self-control. Against such things there is no law. Those who belong to Christ Jesus have crucified the sinful nature with its passions and desires."

The precondition for the Holy Spirit to produce fruit in your life is the death of the sinful nature. You lack significant life-change because you have not put to death the sinful nature. It still reigns in your life. You can dispute it, deny it, or explain it away; but the fruit is the test of your surrender. The Holy Spirit's actions in your life produce godliness. On the other hand, the works of the sinful nature produce fruit that is destructive and hateful.

Putting to Death the Sinful Nature

How do you put to death the sinful nature? Do you kill it with sheer willpower, a dogged determination not to let your baser instincts rule your life? I can tell you from personal experience that willpower has been thoroughly tested and found wanting. Even the strongest of wills, when confronted with unmanageable pressure, will succumb.

So often, people view people with disorders, overeating problems, drug and alcohol addiction, etc. as weak-willed, unable, because of their weaknesses, to lead a balanced life. Nothing could be further from the truth. After spending over twenty-seven years working with addicts, I have concluded that they are some of the most strong-willed individuals you will ever meet.

The strength of their wills can withstand almost every effort to break the strongholds of sin that were the original causes of their addiction. Their stubborn wills block out any help that might set them free. No, you cannot put to death the sinful nature by just wanting it. If you count on determination and personal strength to overcome the sinful nature, you will eventually conclude that the fruit of the Spirit and a changed life is not possible for you.

You might decide to do a word study on the exact meaning of each component of the fruit of the Spirit. In other words, you believe that possessing an abundance of information on a topic will automatically produce positive change in your life. Many in our culture have concluded that education is the cure for all the ills of society and our personal lives. Hence, the bookshelves of the local bookstores are stacked full of self-help books purporting to give us the facts necessary to change our lives.

Without diminishing the virtues of learning or blessing ignorance, I believe that extensive knowledge of the Bible does not necessarily defeat the works of the flesh in a person's life. Unfortunately, we humans share the same tragic fate of living far beneath our education and learning. Circumstances and pain usually trump knowledge and understanding.

Godliness Training Is Not a Homework Assignment

That brings us full circle to the point of this chapter. How can you train yourself to be godly? Godliness training is a daily discipline of Bible meditation, reading, and prayer. It also includes such disciplines as fasting, listening to sermons, godly relationships, and church attendance. "Nothing new," you say. After all, many folks read the Bible every day, attend church, pray, and practice other such disciplines. Despite all of their efforts, so often, unfortunately, the result of all this work is not transformation, but instead, first place in a Bible- trivia contest.

The biggest problem that most people have with Bible reading and practicing a devotional life is their view of Bible reading and devotions. There is a tendency to treat these disciplines as homework. They are assignments that we must complete that satisfy the requirements of a school class. Bible reading becomes an end in and of itself instead of a means to deepen a person's relationship with God.

Instead of treating devotions as an assignment, reading the Bible as a daily chore, you must regard your daily devotions as sacred moments of worship, a special time of intimacy with God. You also must have a plan, a daily training schedule that keeps you on track, which helps you continually surrender your fragmented life to Christ. As you yield your life, you make room for the Holy Spirit to continue working in your life, to produce the fruit that only he can create.

For most people, change is impossible because they do not want to change. In reality, the only change they are hoping to achieve is the consequences of their actions, leaving the source of the problem intact, for to attack the source means discovering something about themselves that they wish to keep hidden. Hardly anyone is willing to believe that he is the source of his character flaws. Blame is easier than change.

In I Timothy 4:7b, the Apostle Paul exhorted Timothy to train himself to be godly. He compared it to training for an athletic event. Anyone who has trained or become an avid fan of a sport knows that greatness, even just competency, takes years to accomplish. Godliness, in much the same way as skill in sports, does not just happen overnight. It is the result of years of training and preparation.

Training Batters the Barriers That Block the Work of the Holy Spirit

The objective of godliness training is to tear down the wall of separation that prevents you from allowing the Holy Spirit to work in your life. The process of becoming a new creature in Christ begins with the transformation and surrender of your mind, that is, the way you think. In Romans 12:1-2 (ESV), we read,

"I appeal to you therefore, brothers, by the mercies of God, to present your bodies as a living sacrifice, holy and acceptable to God, which is your spiritual worship. Do not be conformed to this world, but be transformed by the renewal of your mind, that by testing you may discern what is the will of God, what is good and acceptable and perfect."

Notice that a changed mind follows a surrendered life. When the Bible talks about offering your body as living sacrifice, it essentially means to surrender your life, to submit your hopes, dreams, plans, and will to the Lordship of Christ. However, because you are a living sacrifice, your tendency is to jump off the altar when the flames get too hot. Like most people, you will find that staying surrendered is almost impossible.

One of the results of being human is that you have become comfortable living a fragmented life. That means you have more than one identity. In the morning, you put on your family personality and get your kids ready for school. On the way to work, you put on your commuter costume, honking at strangers, breaking the speed-limit laws, losing your composure and patience because of traffic jams. When you arrive at work, you put on your work identity, climbing the ladder of success, playing office or factory floor politics, and gossiping about the person in the next cubicle. You also wear your church identities, your social identities, your relaxation and entertainment identities, your student identities, your relationship identities. The list is almost endless. You must surrender all these identities to Christ.

Identities not surrendered to Christ create a conflict in your personality that prevents real change from taking place. As previously stated, the Holy Spirit will not work in an area of your life that remains under your control. Your continued control in effect blocks out the work of the Holy Spirit in your life.

Godliness training lowers the barriers of resistance you have erected to protect yourself from pain or knowledge that exposes you to the truth about yourself. It opens the door for the Holy Spirit, effectively giving him permission to work in your life and produce Christ-like fruit. Unfortunately, many habits and flaws are so deeply entrenched, so much a part of the essence of your personality that you simply cannot let go and surrender them to God. That means you have blocked the Holy Spirit from delivering you from their grip. Godliness training will shake them loose and allow God to remove them from your life.

Surrender is more than mouthing words and phrases, more than kneeling at an altar, more than tears, more than a confession. Sometimes, it takes years for you to surrender your rule over parts of your domain unconditionally. Often surrender is like the slow dripping of a faucet, not very perceptible at first, but over time, it overflows the bucket and saturates everything within range.

Begin the process of change today, by setting aside a predetermined amount of time each day dedicated to building your relationship with God. Your daily commitment to spend time with him will change your life.

Part Six: Action Steps for Beating Addiction

You can possess lots of information about a topic without adequately understanding how to use that data to better your life. That is the difference between head knowledge and practical experience. I can tell you everything you need to know about hammering a nail. That does not mean that when I pick up a hammer, I will hit the nail.

When I was in Bridgeport, Connecticut, we had a soup kitchen on the east side of the city. Six nights a week, men, women, boys, and girls would file into the dining room looking for a hot meal. As far as I know, we never disappointed them.

One night, a young man in his late twenties walked into the kitchen. Although he did not come to the kitchen very often, I recognized him immediately. He was one of the drug dealers who practiced his craft on his front porch several doors down from my house.

A couple of days before, my wife complained to me about his activities. Typically, we ignored drug dealers, but this one caught my wife's attention. Several days earlier, the dealer's mother told her she was afraid to leave the house because of all the drug activity on her front porch. My wife asked me to do something about it.

When this young man walked into the kitchen, he immediately spotted me and made a beeline for my position. As soon as he got close, he burst out in a song:

> What a friend we have in Jesus,
> All our sins and griefs to bear!
> What a privilege to carry everything to God in prayer!

Although I was enjoying his singing voice (much better than my own), I interrupted his serenade with these words: "If Jesus were your friend, you and your friends would stop scaring your mother with all your drug dealing in front of your house." Looking down towards the ground, he sheepishly replied, "You got me on that one, Rev." He knew the facts about Jesus. What he knew had little influence over the way he lived his life.

Most of us are like this young man; our knowledge of what is genuine and right is ground down by the pressures and temptations of daily living. Are you like this young man? Does your wisdom exceed your actions?

So far, I have given you some valuable information on beating addiction and changing your life. Now I am going to give you some concrete action steps that will enable you to overthrow your addiction and get your life back.

If you follow my recommendations, you will be on the verge of a brand-new life. If you do not, you will have no one to blame for your defeat but yourself. You will not be able to blame anyone else. If you are serious about getting your life back, it is time to get started.

Action Step One: Connect With God

You must begin today by connecting or reconnecting with God. Only God can give you the strength you need for permanently chasing addiction from your life. Otherwise, you will find yourself facing the same failures and relapses repeatedly. Let us end it today.

You might say, "I'm not a religious sort of person." However, I am not talking about religion. I am talking about a relationship with God.

Here are some facts you need to know:

- God wants to have a relationship with you. To make that happen, he sent his Son, Jesus Christ.
- God's plan for you was never about addiction or ruining your life. His plan for you has always been about helping you reach your full potential and living a meaningful and productive life.
- You wrecked that plan by deciding to go your way and excluding him from your life. The results were catastrophic.
- The life that you are now living is what it means to live a life without God, a sort of living death. You must not blame God or anyone else for the decisions you made. You need to own the life you are now living.
- Despite all you have done, God still loves you and has not given up on you. Everyone else may have lost faith in you, but not God.
- When Jesus died on the cross, he paid the price for your rebellion. He made a way for you to reconnect with him, to give you another chance of fulfilling your real destiny.
- For you to take advantage of this second chance, you must surrender your life to him. In other words, you must give him full control over your life.

Here is what it means to surrender:

- God is first in your life, not second or third.
- His priorities are now your priorities.
- Utilizing his strength in your life, you are now determined to live your life in obedience to him.
- You will begin the process of fulfilling his plan for your life.

To have a relationship with God, you must:

- Admit that your life is in rebellion against God.
- Believe that Christ died and paid the price for your sins.
- Be willing to turn from your old life and embrace the new life of a Christ-follower.
- Surrender your life to Christ.

If you would like to surrender your life to Christ, you may begin by praying this prayer or one like it:

My Heavenly Father, I know that I have made a mess of my life and rebelled against your authority over me. I now give up my old life and turn it over to you. Thank You that Jesus died for my sins so that I might have a relationship with you. Make me into a new person. In the name of Jesus, I pray. Amen.

Before the next hour ends, tell someone you have surrendered your life to Christ. Do not be ashamed. Your surrender is the beginning of your new life.

If you do not have a Bible, make sure you get one right away. In the meantime, you can find Bibles on the internet you can read online. Start your reading with the Gospel of Luke.

This first action step is essential for your success. Otherwise, your only option will be a therapeutic or medical model that will have little chance of attainment.

My wife is currently working as a Registered Nurse in a local detox hospital. She has told me that almost no one ever gets well.

The same men and women recycle in and out of the facility, each time a little worse off than before.

Sometimes, because of their sympathy and compassion for someone wrecked by addiction, people will try desperate measures to help someone get clean. So many of these places ignore God and doom their clients to a life of endless relapse.

As well intentioned as they are, do not listen to them. Even if they do help you, the best that you can expect is that your disease will be in remission. You will have to spend your life in some form of outpatient treatment for the rest of your life.

That is not how God works! With God, your addiction is not just temporarily defeated; he hurls into outer darkness, permanently eradicated from your life. You do not have to focus the rest of your life on staying clean. Once you are clear of addiction, your focus is on growing spiritually in Christ, raising a family, working a job, and living his plan for your life.

All of this starts with a decision, a decision that only you can make. You have to decide that today is the day for you to do the right thing—the right choice for you, for your family and friends, and for you community.

The first time I met Ashley, she was just coming down off heroin. She had spent the last month living in someone's garage, sleeping on a concrete floor. Her addiction had devastated her life.

Things too horrible to mention happened to Ashley while she was in that garage. It seemed as if the whole world had abandoned her.

She was thin the first time I saw her. It took her several weeks to feel physically better after she finished her detox. Sometime during her first month in our program, she made a decision to give her life to Christ. It was a decision that she did not take lightly.

Her sense of physical well-being did not last. She started feeling sick; her strength seemed almost entirely depleted. She put on a lot of excess weight, much faster than average. No matter how much she rested, she did not get any better. We decided to take her to the doctor.

The doctor identified her problem as advanced hepatitis C. The doctor told her that she had less than a year to live. We all began to pray.

Ashley had two beautiful daughters who lived with family members. I asked her if she wanted to go home and spend her last days with her children. Her response was inspiring.

"I want to finish my program. If I go home now, I will probably relapse. I want my children to remember me doing right, not as some drugged-out addict. At least here, I know I will stay clean. My kids' final memory of me will be good and not bad."

Ashley had made a decision to get her life back on track; nothing was going to stop that from happening. Today, Ashley is married and still clean. The doctors could never explain her miraculous healing from Hepatitis C. We knew it was God.

Today is the day for you to get serious. Quit playing with your life. We do not want to lose you. You are too valuable. Please do not waste your life. Give it to Christ.

Action Step One Summary

1) Surrender your life to Christ.
2) Start reading the Gospel of Luke
3) Begin talking to God.

Action Step Two: Take Responsibility for Your Life

Accept responsibility for your life. Your life today is the result of decisions you made in the past. The decisions you make today will determine what kind of life you live in the future.

I am going to ask you a series of questions that will help you understand the exact nature of your past decisions and how they may be affecting you today. Before I do that, let me share with you some good news: God is more than willing to forgive you for your past decisions and wrongdoing. Here is a verse from the Bible:

"If we confess our sins, he is faithful and just and will forgive us our sins and purify us from all unrighteousness."
I John 1:9 (ESV)

In other words, you have to face up to the truth about yourself and your actions and then admit your wrongdoing. When you take responsibility for your behavior, it is an acknowledgment that your behavior was wrong, and you do not plan to do it again. (Do not worry; sometimes we have to work on these issues for some time before we are free from them.)

In admitting your wrongdoing, do not be anxious about God rejecting you. You are not giving him any information about you that he does not already know. In reality, God uses your confession as a means to take your relationship with him to a higher level. He uses it to help change your life.

Let us begin the process. Write down your answers to my questions in a notebook so that you can refer to them later.

1) Do you remember the first time you used drugs or alcohol? In several paragraphs, describe what you were thinking at the time.
2) What are some things that trigger you to use or drink?

3) Describe your relationship with your family. How has addiction influenced your relationship with them?
4) Has your addiction affected your job? If so, please explain the effect your addiction had on your job.
5) Who is to blame for your addiction? Why?

Recently I experienced a catastrophic business failure that left me deeply in debt. Many of my friends tried to comfort me and assure me that it was not my fault. Here is what they said:

- It was the economy.
- Your board members did not help you enough.
- It is not your fault.
- One of your employees undermined you.
- The public just could not catch the vision.

I appreciate the loyalty of my friends, but they were all wrong. Everything they said was true, but ultimately I was to blame for the failure. I was the one who made the decisions that caused the business to fail. Other companies, some similar to mine, faced the exact circumstances and succeeded.

If I had accepted their analysis of my failure, I would have missed a great opportunity to learn something important about business and me. In other words, if I blamed other people or circumstances for my business failure, I would have doomed myself to repeating the same mistakes in my next business venture. My refusal to own my failure would result in the failure of my next venture.

I decided that I needed to learn everything possible about the decisions and actions I took that led to my downfall. I did not want to spend the rest of my life as a failure. I knew that without a fundamental understanding of the nature of my failure, I would end up living my life in a permanent state of failure.

Owning my last fiasco has been a real educational experience. As I look back at my previous venture, I find it hard to believe I could have ever made so many ignorant decisions. That failed undertaking has totally changed the way I think about doing business and building a company.

In the same way, when you own your past mistakes and decide to learn everything you can from them, it changes the way you think about life. In one sense, owning and learning from failure can be a life-changing experience. My life today is far better than the life I use to live. I owe my new life to the lessons I learned from failure.

Until you own your addiction, you will stay an addict for the rest of your life. It might even kill you. If you face up to the fact that your addiction is not the fault of anyone but yourself, you will be on your way to beating substance abuse and getting your life back.

Spend a few moments with God, and tell him it is your fault. He will forgive you.

Action Step Two Summary

1) Make a list of all the damages you have done because of your addiction.
2) Own them.
3) Make a list of what your mistakes have taught you about yourself.

Action Step Three: Find a Church

Part of connecting with God involves connecting with his people. Most of the time when we are trying to overcome our addiction, we spend a great deal of our time connecting with individuals who have the same problems as we do. Unfortunately, when your primary focus is entirely on your addiction, you can lose sight of life's big picture.

An important part of your recovery is restoring normalcy to your life. If your entire focus is addiction, then addiction still owns us. Once your addiction is behind you, the rest of your life will be about family, work, friendships, helping others, and God. Postponing normalcy until a later date will leave you ill prepared to face the challenges associated with your new lifestyle. That is why so few people completely recover from addiction.

Here is how finding and attending a church can help you:

- You will learn more about God than you could on your own.
- You will make friends outside of the recovery culture that will help you transition to a regular life.
- Relationship with other Christians will strengthen your walk with God.
- You will have opportunities to help people in need and involve your life in something bigger than yourself.
- You will experience spiritual growth that will produce more staying power.
- It provides accountability in your life.
- The Christian community is a critical component of God's plan for changing your life.

When it comes to connecting with a church, there are many kinds of churches from which to choose. You may have to try several before you find one that meets your needs. An important thing for you to remember is that your needs are not limited to things that are fun or make you happy. Of course, the church you attend should be able to meet some of your personal needs.

What should you look for in a church? Here is a basic list:

- The Bible must be the central focus of the pastor's sermons.
- The people in the church must be friendly and accepting.
- It must have a stable, active small-group structure to help you connect with people and grow spiritually.
- It needs to have opportunities for you to be involved in ministries outside the walls of the church.
- Because addiction has created serious problems in your life, it must have an addiction program like Celebrate Recovery or something similar.
- Find a church where the music is to your liking and taste.

Once you find a church, set up an appointment to meet with the pastor or one of the staff. Share with the pastor your past struggles and your current needs. Ask for help in finding a mentor in the church who can help you reach the next level in your life.

Once you find a church, be faithful in your attendance. Volunteer for one of the outreach ministries. Attend a small group and the addiction meetings. Get involved.

Get involved in a church immediately. Your future depends on it.

Action Step Three Summary

1) Pick a church to attend this Sunday. If your friends go to church, find out if their church has the programs necessary for your recovery. If so, attend with them.
2) Look up the website of the church. If it does not have what you need, find another.
3) Do as much research as you can about the church before attending. You need to settle into a permanent church home as quickly as possible.

4. Make sure you meet with the pastor.

www.winningtheaddictionbattle.com

Action Step Four: Develop a Daily Devotional Plan

Private time with God is an essential part of your recovery and spiritual growth. Your connectedness with God and your personal growth as a person are your responsibility. Without a daily plan for spending time with God, you will stagnate and probably relapse.

Some individuals, perhaps only a few, have a disposition that allows them to spend hours in spontaneous prayer, without structure or plan. Some describe this as following the lead of the Spirit. Many of us cannot relate to someone who can pray for hours without structure. For us, spontaneity leads to heavy eyelids, a wandering mind, frustration, and eventual defeat. I have spent many hours sleeping on my knees.

Shortly after I became a Christian, someone told me about the importance of having a daily devotional life. The whole idea of spending time with God on a daily basis fascinated me. It was in those beginning months of being a new Christian that a friend gave me a copy of a book detailing the life of George Muller. George Muller was a man who lived in the nineteenth century, founded, and ran homes for orphans. During his long life, God used him to care for thousands of children.

Despite all the good works that he accomplished, George was a man of prayer. He trusted God to supply all their needs, including feeding and caring for the children. Each day, he spent long hours on his knees reading the Bible and praying.

After reading the story of his life, I was inspired to follow him in his devotion to Christ. At the time, I was serving as a U.S. paratrooper in Vicenza, Italy. Once I decided to begin having daily devotions, I made plans to start the following morning. My usual wakeup time was 5:00 a.m. Therefore, I decided to get up at 4:30 and spend thirty minutes doing my devotions.

The next morning, I sprang out of bed at 4:30. I was excited and filled with anticipation. I got on my knees and began to pray. Within a few minutes, I started having difficulty concentrating on my prayers. My mind began to wander, drifting along with each random thought that interrupting my prayers. I did not regain consciousness until they woke me up at five o'clock.

I wish I could say that after a few more days of struggling, I had an emotionally rewarding prayer experience. I did not! Although I was able to concentrate when I read and studied the Bible, prayer continued to be a challenging and trying endeavor. I loved the idea of prayer, yet I never could master the exercise. For many years, instead of praying, I read books about prayer. When I did pray, I prayed that God would help me discover the secret of having a daily devotional life. I knew if I figured out how to pray, it would have a significant impact on my life.

In my early thirties, I found myself in charge of a small mission in North Carolina. The place was wild. Most of the men at the mission had been in and out of the mission for over ten years.

I sat at the front desk each night. My primary responsibility on the desk was to watch for men who returned to the mission under the influence of alcohol. Almost every night someone came back to the mission drunk. When I would confront them about their drunkenness, they would erupt with abusive threats and accusations against my character. Often I would have to call the police to have them removed from the premises.

At first, their behavior was very confusing to me. After all, while at the mission, they were required to attend the morning, afternoon, and evening Bible studies. They also had access to trained counselors to help them process through their issues. I thought that if I exposed them to enough Bible teaching and preaching, their lives would transform into something beyond their current situations.

I saw little in the way of real and lasting transformation in their lives. I hope I planted seeds in their lives that will someday bear real fruit. In the meantime, must they be condemned to live lives of continuous setbacks and failures, suffering without meaning and despair without hope?

In my life, I had seen some progress, some meaningful change in my condition, yet my setbacks were so tumultuous, so devastating and painful, that I often was overwhelmed with guilt and remorse. I felt trapped, a victim of my defects and character flaws. I understood the frustration of the Apostle Paul when he cried out, "Wretched man that I am. Who will deliver me from this body of death?" (Romans 7:24, ESV)

I did all the usual, regular disciplines most Christians performed. I attended church on Sundays, read and studied my Bible, and read many helpful Christian books. Of course, I continued reading books on prayer.

I still tried to have a meaningful devotional life. I knew that if I ever hoped to overcome myself, to have a deeper relationship with God and become godly in my character, I would somehow have to transcend my lack of progress in this area.

In my desire to help the men and women who knocked on my door almost every day looking for help, I kept searching for a method or technique to help them become successful. Over time, I discovered the devotional writings of the early Christians. It seemed as though the men and women who had written these manuscripts understood me.

Based on some of the things I learned from them, I began to experiment on me and the men and women in my programs. It took about ten years to develop a devotional program that helped me start to change in a more significant way. I also began to see some additional progress in the lives of the men and women who were the primary focus of my work.

Perhaps your daily devotions fail to measure up to your expectations. Just as I did for many years, you have tried to have a consistent, regular devotional life but have failed as often as you have tried. Instead of having to deal with the guilt associated with failure, you gave up. You decided you lacked the proper temperament that made praying and meditating on God's Word possible.

Do not give up yet. Here are just some of the benefits you will experience from your daily devotions:

- You will have a clearer understanding of God's will for your life.
- Closely related, you will have a greater knowledge of the Scriptures, enabling you to have a better sense of direction and guidance from God for decisions you need to make to live your life.
- Over time, you will begin to change, to become more godly and Christ-like.
- Your wisdom will mature and grow.
- You will be able to weather the storms, both spiritually and emotionally, that will most certainly come into your life.
- Setbacks and failures will not destroy you.
- You will have a more confident and happier perspective on your life.
- God will be your friend.
- You will learn to embrace surrender and brokenness.
- No matter what is happening in your life, you will trust in the power, love, and wisdom of God.
- Your friends, family, and coworkers will notice a difference in you.
- Your pride will gradually diminish, replaced by humility and service.
- Your life will grow bigger and stronger.
- You will win your battle against addiction.

If your desire is to fulfill God's purpose for your life, then you must begin the practice of having a daily devotion.

What you need is a plan designed to keep your mind occupied and focused. To accomplish that, you need structure and a path to follow. Thank goodness, it was not necessary to invent something new. Church history is replete with examples and instruction on how to have daily communion with God.

The time that you spend with God is indicative of the priority you place on your relationship with Him. If you say that you are too busy with work, family, hobbies, or even your church activities to spend quantity time with God on a daily basis, then your very words have clearly spelled out the low priority you have placed on your relationship with him. You spend time pursuing the things that are important to you.

Although the Bible does not clearly spell out how much time you should spend with God each day, it is clear that your daily activities are to place him supreme in all of your undertakings and thoughts. The time you spend with him cannot be limited to a few moments squeezed between scattered bits of activities and commitments. Like a date with someone you love, you should carefully plan the time, place, and activities for your daily appointment with God.

The Word of God is the primary tool the Holy Spirit uses to change and transform your life.

That is why your date should always include meaningful time for reading, meditating, and praying the Word. These disciplines will ultimately lead to a more Christ-like character that increasingly produces the fruit of the spirit.

First, you must block out, at least, one hour a day for your daily devotions. If you want to change, overcome character issues, beat addiction, and experience the presence and power of God in your everyday life, you will learn to view spending an hour in the presence of God as a privilege instead of a sacrifice.

The schedule consists of five parts:

1) A daily devotional reading

2) Meditation on a Scripture verse
3) Prayer rooted in Scripture
4) Prayer
5) Bible reading

Many people are unable to spend more than few moments with God because they lack a structured format that is both useful and meaningful. In the beginning, a well-thought-out format may seem mechanical, perhaps even too structured. That is because the program is new and unfamiliar. It will soon begin to flow and feel more natural as you become more competent in your daily devotions.

Because you lived such an undisciplined life while trapped in your addiction, you may find this routine even harder than the average person might. You must decide right now just how badly you want to defeat addiction and get your life back. Your answer will determine your course of action.

You should not wait until you are ready to start. Emotionally you may never be ready. So get with it, and begin right now. Follow this basic outline:

Opening Prayer

Open your time with God with prayer. Your prayer should include the following:

- Praise for who he is
- Things you are grateful for
- Confession of sin
- A request for guidance during your devotion
- A general surrender of your life to Him
- A daily devotional reading

Devotional Reading

At the back of this book, you will find a list of books that I recommend for you to use in your daily devotions. Each day you should read a section of your chosen book. Limit your time to about fifteen minutes.

As you read, ask God to speak to you. Pray that he will use this devotion for making you more like Christ. Do not be in a hurry!

Scripture Meditation

In Psalm 1:2, we read,

"But his delight is in the law of the Lord; and on his law he meditates day and night."

For years, I have used a simple format in my devotional life and my life-change programs. It keeps me focused. I use a spiral notebook, one page per devotion. You can use this format on any verse in the Bible, but I primarily use it for Psalms or Proverbs. Each day I select just one verse for my meditation. In my notebook, I write down my response to the following instructions or questions:

1) Copy the verse from the Bible that is the focus of today's meditation.
2) Using your words, rephrase the verse to make its meaning clearer.
3) What is the teaching of the verse? What is it trying to say?
4) What does the verse say to you personally?
5) What changes do you have to make in your life because of this meditation?

This meditation will help you focus on God and deepen your surrender to him.

Scripture Prayer

The best method for keeping your prayers focused on God and his direction for your life is using the Bible as your prayer book. Scripture prayer is an ancient form of prayer used by Christians for deepening their connection with God. I use it primarily for praying verse by verse through the New Testament. I skip the genealogies.

Here is an outline for you to use as you pray through the Scriptures:

1. Select a passage of Scripture to read. Slowly read the passage of Scripture, thinking and listening as you read. When a phrase or verse stands out to you, begin to repeat that verse over and over again, as though you were attempting to memorize it.
2. As you read, ask yourself these questions:
    - What is God trying to say to me?
    - What does this passage say about me?
    - Do I need to make any changes in me?
    - Does this passage require anything of me today?
3. Based on the answers to the questions, begin to pray to God.
4. Listen to the quiet voice of God for about fifteen seconds. Listen to what God is trying to say to you through this verse.

Once you pick a phrase or verse, you should focus on it using the above structure for just several minutes. Then continue to read until another passage or phrase stands out, and then repeat the exercise. Do this for about ten minutes.

Daily Bible Reading

The best way to read the Bible is to buy a Bible with a daily reading plan that, if followed, will bring you through the entire Bible in one year. If you prefer to use your own Bible, the internet is full of daily Bible reading plans that you can follow. A daily Bible-reading plan ensures that you read the whole Bible, not just your favorite parts.

Do not treat your daily Bible readings as an assignment to be completed. Remember, as you read, you are interacting with the Creator of the universe. God desperately wants to have a relationship with you. Do not cheapen it by being in a hurry and treating it as a duty instead of a date with your most special friend in the world. If you need more time to complete your Bible reading, set apart some time later in the day to finish your reading.

Closing Prayer

Spend the last few minutes of your devotional time praying for your needs and the needs of others. Buy yourself another spiral notebook. Draw a line down the middle of the page. On the left side of the line, write down your prayer request and the date. When God answers your prayer, record the answer and the date in the right column across from the corresponding prayer.

This method will help you in two ways. Firstly, it will provide you with a list of all the things you have committed to pray for, ensuring that you continue praying for a particular problem, person, or need until God answers your prayer. Secondly, you will eventually have a written record of God's answers to your prayers. In a world that questions the value of prayer, your notebook will be proof that God still hears and answers your prayers.

Conclusion

Now you have a basic outline of a daily devotional plan that has been tested and proven powerful and life changing. Unfortunately, no shortcut exists that gives you overnight success in personal transformation. As a journey begins with the first step, so you, too, must take the first step in fulfilling God's destiny for your life.

God has a bigger plan for you than your present life. To fulfill that fate, you must be willing to spend time with him each day. If you could have changed yourself without living in the presence of God, you would have already done so.

God wants to have a relationship with you. A relationship is not just the acceptance of a gift; a relationship is a product of significant and quality time spent on a regular and consistent basis with God.

Action Step Four Summary

1. Set up all the materials you will need to have a daily devotion.
2. Pick out a consistent time for your devotions.

3. Go to my website at winningtheaddictionbattle.com for videos and other helps.

Action Step Five: Start a Mastermind Group

The purpose of a mastermind group is two-fold:
1) To help you achieve your vision for your life
2) To help the rest of your team realize their visions for their lives

It is a truism that no one succeeds in life without the aid of others. It is also true that no one succeeds in life without helping others achieve their goals.

To beat addiction, you must develop a plan for your life. This plan must include the following details:

- What you want your family relationships to look like in five years
- Your goals for your career
- Vision for making a difference in the world

Your mastermind group should not consist of more than five people, preferably of the same gender. If your group is too large, you will lose focus and dilute its effectiveness. If you mix the sexes, you will set yourself up for disaster.

You should meet once a week. At the meetings, each person should share with the group their goals and plans for achieving them. The group should then discuss each member's goals and plans, offer suggestions, and provide constructive criticism. The purpose is to increase the chance of success for members by helping them refine, enhance, and make positive adjustments in each of their plans.

Starting a Mastermind Group

Start with one person. Between the two of you, decide on another person to invite into your group. Once you have a third person, the three of you decide on who your fourth person should be. Continue doing this until your team is full.

It is important that you recruit members who are motivated to succeed; otherwise, your meetings will be a waste of your time. Your mastermind group meeting is not a recovery meeting. Your group is not just about staying clean and sober; it is about building a significant and fruitful life. It will also help you in your efforts to defeat addiction by focusing on your life beyond dependency.

Before asking someone to join your group, ask them the following questions:

- What do you hope to gain by joining this group?
- Are you willing to commit to meeting one day each week?
- Have you set any goals for your life?
- Have you formulated an action plan to help you achieve these objectives?
- Are you willing to receive constructive criticism without getting defensive?
- Are you ready to help me achieve my goals?

Spend a few minutes sharing your goals and dreams with your perspective member. Listen to their story without interruption. Do you think this person will be a good fit for your life? Are you a good fit for his or her life?

If you are not the only member, both of you must be in full agreement about inviting someone into your group. Consensus is mandatory.

Meeting Details

Although there is no hard and fast rule, the most efficient mastermind groups meet once a week for about an hour. Here is a basic outline of the meeting:

1) Each member details their progress in accomplishing the weekly goal they shared with the group at the previous session. The other members give constructive feedback and encouragement.

2) Each week a different member of the group is on the hot seat. The member shares with the group details about their goals, including the progress they are making and the difficulties they are facing in implementing their goals. He or she shares significant problems and successes. It is also a time for that person to ask for constructive advice. The other members give feedback, advice, helpful criticism, and encouragement.
3) Each member shares with the group, at least, one primary goal they hope to accomplish by the next meeting.

Your mastermind members are a critical component of your future success. They help you get your mind off your addiction and start creating your future. If you do that, your life will be successful on multiple levels.

Action Step Five Summary

1) Ask your pastor for help in recruiting your first member.
2) Set up a meeting with that person.
3) After you recruit your first person, have a meeting.
4) Continue recruiting until your group is full.
5) For more information on Mastermind Groups, go to my website at winningtheaddictionbattle.com.

A Call to Action

It was the early eighties. I was sitting in church one Sunday, listening attentively to the pastor's sermon. Although I was paying attention to what he said, I honestly cannot remember the details of his sermon.

I do remember the details concerning my messed-up life. I was just coming out of another relapse. Relapse was a pattern for me, something that I just could not shake. No matter how hard I tried, I did not have the staying power to remain sober. I was sure that I would not relapse again; but then again, there was this pattern thing, the continuous free-fall into self-destruction that doomed all my efforts to succeed.

My life was one perpetual excuse, packed with reasons that explained my failures. I could not accept the fact that I might be responsible for my reversals. It was always someone else's fault. Those who would not buy into my relapse excuses made me furious.

That Sunday morning sermon altered everything. It was only one sentence in the sermon. "A genuine measure of a man's greatness can be determined by what it takes to frustrate him from doing God's will for his life." It was as though someone drove a knife deep into my gut. "I'm not very great. It doesn't take much to frustrate me," I thought. It was my decisive moment.

I realized that my principal enemy was myself. No one else had the capability of wrecking my life as thoroughly as I could. My relapses were not the product of some outside force, some evil person who had plotted my demise. My relapses happened because I wanted them to happen. I was not willing to pay the price a new life would cost me.

That day was the end of my old life. I never relapsed again. Since that day, my life has profoundly changed. I do not always succeed at everything I try, yet I rarely blame others for my mistakes. Excuses never have a good outcome.

Are you ready to step up to the plate?

Now you have a plan for defeating addiction and changing the whole direction of your life. You no longer have to settle, to be content with mediocrity and low expectations. You actually can become all that God wants you to be. For that to happen, you must begin now. The actions you take today will determine the future you live tomorrow. What will you do?

Sign Up for Free Materials to Help you in
Your Battle with Your Addiction.
www.winningtheaddictionbattle.com

Suggested Books

Devotional

1) My Utmost for His Highest by Oswald Chambers
2) Holiness Day by Day: Transformational Thoughts for Your Spiritual Journey (Hardcover) by Jerry Bridges
3) The Return of the Prodigal Son: A Story of Homecoming (Paperback) by Henri J.M. Nouwen
4) A Shepherd Looks at Psalm 23 (Paperback) by W. Phillip Keller
5) Don't Waste Your Life (Paperback) by John Piper
6) Trusting God: Even When Life Hurts (Paperback) by Jerry Bridges
7) Jesus: 90 Days With the One and Only (Personal Reflections) by Beth Moore
8) David: 90 Days with A Heart Like His (Personal Reflections Series) by Beth Moore
9) Paul: 90 Days on His Journey of Faith (Personal Reflections) by Beth Moore
10) John: 90 Days with the Beloved Disciple (Personal Reflections) by Beth Moore
11) The Tender Words of God by Ann Spangler

Success

1) Over the Top: Moving from Survival to Stability, from Stability to Success, from Success to Significance by Zig Ziglar
2) Zig Ziglar's Life Lifters: Moments of Inspiration for Living Life Better by Zig Ziglar How to Win Friends and Influence People by Dale Carnegie
3) The 7 Habits of Highly Effective People by Stephen R. Covey
4) As A Man Thinketh by James Allen
5) The Greatest Salesman in the World by Og Mandino

About Jim Watson

Jim Watson has spent the last twenty-seven years helping men and women trapped in addiction get their lives back!

Jim has opened six missions across the country that specializes in addiction recovery. He spent years and over one million dollars developing programming and systems that can help you defeat addiction and fulfill God's purpose for your life.

For me, addiction is personal. During my twenties, I wrecked my life because of my addiction to alcohol.

My brother's addiction to alcohol ruined his life and then killed him. Helping you win your battle with addiction is not just a profession; it is a life-mission.

At one point in my life, I was the last person you would have expected to become a minister. I was wild and crazy, hell-bent on wrecking my life. Because of my addiction to alcohol, I could not hold a job, pay my bills or succeed at personal relationships. I was a loser. No matter how hard I tried to stay sober, I always relapsed. I could not find a way out of my addiction.

Eventually, I grew tired of inflicting so much pain and destruction upon myself. I surrendered my life to Christ. That was the beginning of the end of my addiction. Unfortunately, beating addiction is more than just uttering a prayer of commitment and attending church on a regular basis. It requires a disciplined lifestyle of prayer, service and community. These personal disciplines opened the door for God's power to enter my life. I have been sober for over thirty-years. Since I surrendered to Christ, my life has never been the same.

What God did for me, he can do for you!

Made in the USA
Charleston, SC
21 April 2016